ISLAMIC
TEACHINGS SERIES

FAITH

ISLAMIC
TEACHINGS SERIES

FAITH

COMPILED FROM THE WORKS OF
SHAYKH-UL-ISLAM DR
MUHAMMAD TAHIR-UL-QADRI

MINHAJ-UL-QURAN PUBLICATIONS

Published by Minhaj-ul-Quran Publications
292-296 Romford Road
London, E7 9HD
United Kingdom

First Published December 2011

www.minhajpublications.com

ISBN: 978-1-908229-05-2

Typeset: Muhammad Farooq Rana

Acknowledgements:
Mrs Farida Sajjad, Misbah Kabeer, Muhammad Farooq Rana, Muhammad Sohail Siddiqui, Waqas Amin, Rafiq Patel, Asma Parveen, Mariam Khalid, Karim Mamdani and all other brothers and sisters involved in this compilation.

Printed in Turkey by Mega Print,Istanbul

Table of Contents

Foreword

Human beings have been created to worship Allah, and have been prescribed to acquire awareness of and sincerity with Him. Acts of worship, as if they are no more than a habit, may earn you reward in the hereafter but give you no support at all for obtaining awareness and spiritual light. The same acts of worship, when they are performed with true, sincere and acute observation of the divine presence,[1] earn you a station of proximity to and feeling of company with the Lord Almighty, where you receive delightful divine enchantments to enkindle your faith as well as reassurance for your soul's aspirations to a place in the divine court in a state of tranquillity and His good pleasure.[2]

Minhaj-ul-Qurʾan International works under the patronage of his eminence, Shaykh-ul-Islam Prof Dr Muhammad Tahir-ul-Qadri and discharges its duties of guiding and uplifting the Muslim Umma at each level.

This book is part of the *Taʿlīmāt Islam* series compiled from the works and lectures of Shaykh-ul-Islam Dr Muhammad Tahir-ul-Qadri. Their aim is to provide readers with both a general overview and where needed, some indepth information and guidance on the basics of

---

1 The reference is to the hadith of Jibrīl where it says that you should worship Allah as if you were seeing Him.

2 The reference is to the verse of the Qurʾan which says: 'O contented (pleased) self! Return to your Lord in such a state that you are both the aspirant to, and the aspired of, His pleasure (i.e., you seek His pleasure and He seeks yours).' [*al-Fajr*, 89:27–28].

Islam. All of the primary subjects within the three branches of the Shariah, *ʿaqīda* (doctrine), *fiqh* (jurisprudence), *tasawwuf* (spirituality and self purification) are covered and a general basic understanding of Islam in a modern context through an easy to follow question and answer format. Some of the most common yet unanswered day to day issues are replied to using juristic methods from sound sources of Quran and hadith.

These are not only of benefit for the purpose of self study, for anybody of any age and from every walk of life, it is also a very useful reference source which caters for the needs of academic institutions, libraries and study circles.

We pray God Almighty to grant us the best of faith and deeds and accept all the services rendered by all the persons involved in bringing about this collection.

Faith

Q.1. What is *Īmān* (faith)?

Ans. *Īmān* means to utter faith in Allah ﷻ and His Messenger ﷺ and all that has been sent to us from Him through His Messenger ﷺ with the tongue and believe that in the heart.

Q.2. What does *Īmān* signify?

Ans. The word *īmān* (إِيْمان) is an Arabic word that comes from the root word (أ، م، ن). Literally, it signifies 'to be safe from all fears, to be at peace in the heart and to accomplish well-being'. When used intransitively, the word *īmān* means to be at peace. When used transitively, it signifies 'providing peace and security'.[3]

Having faith in somebody means to testify to him and to trust in his truthfulness beyond doubt. So, the word *īmān*, in its real sense, stands for security, trust and faith.

Q.3. What is the reality of faith?

Ans. *Īmān* is a state of certainty in the heart and soul that empties them of love for the lower world and fills them with divine love. The following hadith explains this very well.

Ḥārith b. Mālik al-Anṣārī ؓ relates that the Prophet ﷺ once asked him as he passed by him ﷺ, 'O Ḥārith!

---

[3] Ibn Manẓūr al-Afrīqī, *Lisān al-ʿArab*, 13:23; and al-Zubaydī, *Tāj al-ʿurūs min jawāhir al-qāmūs*, 18:23–24.

How was your morning?' He replied, 'O Allah's Messenger! I had a morning prosperous with the reality of faith.' He ﷺ said, 'O Ḥārith! Consider what you say. Everything has a reality. So, what is the true essence of your faith? (What do you mean when you say that you have obtained the actual faith?) He replied, 'O Allah's Messenger! I have detached myself from the love of worldliness; I stay up worshipping at night and keep myself thirsty (in fasting) during the daytime. [So, I have obtained a state of my soul] as if I (literally) observe the Divine Throne with my naked eyes; (as if) I see the inhabitants of Paradise visiting one another; (as if) I see the people of Hell falling upon one another in Fire.' The Prophet ﷺ said, 'O Ḥārith, you have become a gnostic. Now retain it firmly.' He ﷺ repeated this thrice.[4]

Q.4. How many times is the word 'Īmān' used in the Qur'ān?

Ans. Approximately 45 times.

Q.5. What falls under the topic of Īmān?

Ans. It is *ʿaqīda* / faith (both elements and articles of faith) – that is also called theology.

Q.6. What is *ʿaqīda*?

Ans. This word comes from the root letters [ع، ق، د] which signify 'to tie a knot'.[5] It is used to describe the verification of something that renders it beyond doubt. It is also used for faith in something as absolute truth. As a term in theology, it means to affirm the realities that have

---

[4] Narrated by Ibn Abī Shayba in *al-Muṣannaf*, 6:170 §30352.

[5] Dr Ibrāhīm Anīs, *al-Muʿjam al-wasīt*, 2:614.

been communicated to us by Allah ﷻ through the office of prophethood beyond the slightest doubt.

Q.7. What is the difference between *īmān* and *ʿaqīda*?

Ans. *ʿAqīda* means to resolve on something firmly in the heart, having faith in it as the absolute truth. *Īmān* is the initial teaching of Islam that requires every Muslim to attest to the truthfulness of Allah ﷻ and His Messenger ﷺ and to believe in them. It is *īmān* when a Muslim affirms that the teachings of Islam are the truth and confirms this in the heart. When the same is settled in his heart firmly and becomes impossible to displace, it is called *ʿaqīda*. So, when *īmān* grows, it becomes *ʿaqīda*. *ʿAqīda* is a mature and firmly resolved form of *īmān*.

Q.8. What is the science of *ʿaqīda* called?

Ans. It is called *ʿilm al-ʿaqāʾid* or *ʿilm al-kalām*.

Q.9. Can the knowledge of something be declared *īmān*?

Ans. No. You do not achieve the heartfelt state of *īmān* only by knowing something. If knowing something could be understood as faith in that thing, then every illiterate person would be an unbeliever and every educated person would be regarded as a believer. Let's not forget that Abū Jahl and his friends used to say:

مِنَّا نَبِيٌّ يَأْتِيْهِ الْوَحْيُ مِنَ السَّمَاءِ، فَمَتَى نُدْرِكُ هَذِهِ؟ ... وَاللهِ لا نُؤْمِنُ بِهِ أَبَداً وَلا نُصَدِّقُهُ.

> We know that there is a Prophet among us who receives the revelation from above (from God). ... By God, we shall never believe in him. Nor shall

> we attest to him (as truthful in proclaiming prophethood).[6]

It is clear from the above that knowledge of something and faith in that thing are two different things. Sometimes, a person does not have faith despite having an education. On the other hand, sometimes a person can have firm faith without an education. Allah ﷻ says of faith:

> ٱلَّذِينَ يُؤْمِنُونَ بِٱلْغَيْبِ.
>
> Those who believe in the unseen.[7]

It also shows that faith means to believe without seeing whereas knowledge means to confirm by sight.

Q.10. What are the articles of *īmān*?

Ans. The leading scholars of the Qur'ān and hadith, as well as their expert interpreters, have derived the significance of *īmān* and defined it in an amiable manner so as to explain it to us in simple terms. They have described it in two ways: *īmān mujmal* (the brief definition of faith) and *īmān mufaṣṣal* (the detailed definition of faith). *Īmān mujmal* defines *īmān* in brief terms and mentions faith in Allah ﷻ in a fashion that includes all the necessary tenets of faith that emanate from a deep and comprehensive study of the Qur'ān and hadith without articulating them as such. *Īmān mufaṣṣal*, on the other hand, covers them all explicitly.

Q.11. What is *īmān mujmal*?

Ans. It is as follows:

---

[6] Narrated by Ibn Kathīr in *Tafsīr al-Qur'ān al-ʿaẓīm*, 2:131.

[7] Qur'ān 2:3.

آمَنْتُ بِاللهِ كَمَا هُوَ بِأَسْمَائِهِ وصِفَاتِهِ وَقَبِلْتُ جَمِيْعَ أَحْكَامِهِ، إِقْرارٌ بِاللِّسَانِ وَتَصْدِيْقٌ بِالْقَلْبِ.

I believe in Allah as He is with all His names and attributes; and I accept all His commands, asserting this by the tongue and confirming it in the heart.

Q.12. What is *Īmān Mufaṣṣal*?

Ans. It is as follows:

آمَنْتُ بِاللهِ وَملائِكَتِهِ وَكُتُبِهِ ورُسُلِهِ والْيَومِ الْآخِرِ والْقَدْرِ خَيْرِهِ وشَرِّهِ مِنَ اللهِ تَعَالَى والْبَعْثِ بَعْدَ الْمَوْتِ.

I believe in Allah, His angels, His books, His Messengers, the Last Day, destiny – both its good and evil – to be from Allah (created by Him) and in resurrection after death.

Q.13. Faith in what articles has been enjoined upon us?

Ans. The following verse of the Qur'ān explains the basic tenets of faith:

يَٰٓأَيُّهَا ٱلَّذِينَ ءَامَنُوٓاْ ءَامِنُواْ بِٱللَّهِ وَرَسُولِهِۦ وَٱلْكِتَٰبِ ٱلَّذِى نَزَّلَ عَلَىٰ رَسُولِهِۦ وَٱلْكِتَٰبِ ٱلَّذِىٓ أَنزَلَ مِن قَبْلُ.

O Believers! Put faith in Allah and His Messenger (ﷺ) and in the Book which He has revealed to His Messenger (ﷺ) and the Book that He revealed before (it).[8]

Another verse also states:

[8] Ibid., 4:136.

ءَامَنَ ٱلرَّسُولُ بِمَآ أُنزِلَ إِلَيْهِ مِن رَّبِّهِۦ وَٱلْمُؤْمِنُونَ كُلٌّ ءَامَنَ بِٱللَّهِ وَمَلَٰٓئِكَتِهِۦ وَكُتُبِهِۦ وَرُسُلِهِۦ.

> (He) the Messenger (ﷺ) believed in (i.e., affirmed) what was revealed to him by his Lord and so did the believers. All embraced faith (from the core of their hearts) in Allah, His angels, His Books and His Messengers.[9]

Further to that, the Prophet ﷺ has also declared it incumbent to believe in the following articles according to the famous hadith of Gabriel (Jibrīl)[10] which is agreed upon (reported by both Imam al-Bukhārī and Imam Muslim):

1. Faith in Allah ﷻ
2. Faith in angels
3. Faith in the heavenly books
4. Faith in the Messengers ﷺ
5. Faith in the Last Day
6. Faith in destiny both good and evil being from Allah

Q.14. What does *Īmān bi Allāh* (faith in Allah) mean?

Ans. *Īmān bi Allāh* means to declare Allah's being one—the unique, the Creator, the Owner, the Cherisher, the Provider and the Sustainer—with the tongue combined with its testimony deep in the heart.

---

[9] Ibid., 2:285.

[10] Narrated by al-Bukhārī in *al-Ṣaḥīḥ: Kitāb al-īmān* [The book of Faith], chapter: 'On the Questioning of Gabriel', 1:27 §50.

Q.15. What are the attributes of Allah?

Ans. The attributes of Allah ﷻ are numerous—beyond counting. They are limitless just as Allah's ﷻ entity knows no boundaries or limits. His attributes, excellence and perfection are beyond comprehension, thought and speech. Below we mention some of these:

1 يَعْلَمُ مَا بَيْنَ أَيْدِيهِمْ وَمَا خَلْفَهُمْ وَلَا يُحِيطُونَ بِهِۦ عِلْمًا.

He knows all those (things) which are ahead of them and which are behind them, and they cannot encompass His (knowledge) with (their) knowledge.[11]

2 لَيْسَ كَمِثْلِهِۦ شَىْءٌ ۖ وَهُوَ ٱلسَّمِيعُ ٱلْبَصِيرُ.

There is nothing like Him and He alone is All-Hearing, All-Seeing.[12]

3 لَّا تُدْرِكُهُ ٱلْأَبْصَٰرُ وَهُوَ يُدْرِكُ ٱلْأَبْصَٰرَ ۖ وَهُوَ ٱللَّطِيفُ ٱلْخَبِيرُ.

No vision can grasp His Sight but He has encompassed all vision and sight. He is the All-Penetrating Viewer, All-Aware.[13]

4 He is the First—meaning that he has no beginning—and the last—meaning that He does not have an end. He is the Evident and the Concealed.

5 Any and every thing other than His divine self has been created by Him. He is the one who annihilates every being and will raise everybody from the dead on the Day of Judgement.

---

[11] Qur'ān 20:110.

[12] Ibid., 42:11.

[13] Ibid., 6:103.

6 He does not need anybody or anything whereas everybody and everything needs His favour.

7 He is not confined to a body or body-like thing and is free of all the qualities that a body can or may have such as eating, drinking, sleeping, etc.

8 He holds control over every being and executes what He pleases.

9 Only He gives life and causes death. Only He inflicts illness and bestows health.

10 Only He confers honour and dignity or brings to disgrace and humiliation. Only He inflicts harm or confers benefit and provides with sustenance.

11 No action that He executes is without wisdom. [Our understanding may well fall short of its conception.]

12 He is the Owner and Custodian of all and the King of kings.

13 Only He deserves worship.

Q.16. Can any of the divine attributes be found in any of His creation?

Ans. Yes! Some of the divine attributes are known as 'general attributes'. These are also found in creation. When they are attributed to Allah ﷻ, they signify their real sense and shall be understood as 'the attributes as they belong to the Divinity'. When they refer to a created entity—such as a human being—they are used metaphorically and are understood as a divine bestowal.

The fact is that the qualities that appear in creation do not resemble those of the Creator in any sense whatsoever. They are rather a conferral of the Lord Almighty. Creatures have been granted these qualities so that they can seek help from them in order to recognise Allah's attributes to the best of their understanding. In other words, the conferral of these qualities is a resource of divine cognition for us. We mention here some of them to clarify the matter.

	Attributes attributed to Allah ﷻ	Same qualities bestowed to creation
1	إِنَّهُۥ هُوَ ٱلسَّمِيعُ ٱلْبَصِيرُ. Surely He is the One Who is All-Hearing, All-Seeing.[14]	فَجَعَلْنَٰهُ سَمِيعًا بَصِيرًا. So We have made him (in the order of) hearing (then) seeing.[15]
2	إِنَّ ٱللَّهَ بِٱلنَّاسِ لَرَءُوفٌ رَّحِيمٌ. Allah is surely Most Clement, Ever-Merciful to mankind.[16]	لَقَدْ جَآءَكُمْ رَسُولٌ مِّنْ أَنفُسِكُمْ عَزِيزٌ عَلَيْهِ مَا عَنِتُّمْ حَرِيصٌ عَلَيْكُم بِٱلْمُؤْمِنِينَ رَءُوفٌ رَّحِيمٌ. Surely a (Glorious) Messenger from amongst yourselves has come to you. Your suffering and distress (becomes) grievously heavy on him ﷺ. (O mankind,) he is ardently desirous of your (betterment and guidance. And) he is most (deeply) clement and merciful to the

[14] Ibid., 17:1.
[15] Ibid., 76:2.
[16] Ibid., 2:143.

	Attributes attributed to Allah ﷻ	Same qualities bestowed to creation
		believers.[17]
3	إِنَّ ٱللَّهَ عَلَىٰ كُلِّ شَيْءٍ شَهِيدٌ. Surely Allah is witnessing everything.[18]	وَيَكُونَ ٱلرَّسُولُ عَلَيْكُمْ شَهِيدًا. And (Our exalted) Messenger bears witness to you.[19]
4	وَكَلَّمَ ٱللَّهُ مُوسَىٰ تَكْلِيمًا. And Allah (also) spoke to Mūsā ([Moses] directly).[20]	Mūsā ﷺ also spoke to Allah directly.
5	أَيَبْتَغُونَ عِندَهُمُ ٱلْعِزَّةَ فَإِنَّ ٱلْعِزَّةَ لِلَّهِ جَمِيعًا. Do they seek honour in their company? So, all veneration (and glory) belongs only to Almighty Allah.[21]	وَلِلَّهِ ٱلْعِزَّةُ وَلِرَسُولِهِۦ وَلِلْمُؤْمِنِينَ وَلَٰكِنَّ ٱلْمُنَٰفِقِينَ لَا يَعْلَمُونَ. But in fact honour belongs to Allah alone and His Messenger and the believers. However, the hypocrites do not understand (this reality).[22]

[17] Ibid., 9:128.
[18] Ibid., 22:17.
[19] Ibid., 2:143.
[20] Ibid., 4:164.
[21] Ibid., 4:139.
[22] Ibid., 63:8.

	Attributes attributed to Allah ﷻ	Same qualities bestowed to creation
6	أَنَّ ٱلْقُوَّةَ لِلَّهِ جَمِيعًا. The Master of all the forces is Allah.[23]	One of the companions of Sulaymān [Solomon] ﷺ said: قَالَ عِفْرِيتٌ مِّنَ ٱلْجِنِّ أَنَا۠ ءَاتِيكَ بِهِۦ قَبْلَ أَن تَقُومَ مِن مَّقَامِكَ ۖ وَإِنِّى عَلَيْهِ لَقَوِىٌّ أَمِينٌ. One mighty jinn submitted: 'I can bring it to you before you rise from your seat. And I am indeed energetic (enough) and trustworthy (to bring it).'[24]
7	بِيَدِكَ ٱلْخَيْرُ. All good is in Your Mighty Hand[25]	وَمَن يُؤْتَ ٱلْحِكْمَةَ فَقَدْ أُوتِىَ خَيْرًا كَثِيرًا. And he who is granted wisdom (and reason) receives tremendous good[26]

[23] Ibid., 2:165.
[24] Ibid., 27:39.
[25] Ibid., 3:26.
[26] Ibid., 2:269.

Q.17. What are the attributes that are specific to the Divine Being?

Ans. They are quite a few. We mention just some of them here:

1. Allah ﷻ alone is the true deity and the only one worthy of worship. We do not have any right at all to associate any being with Him in the matter of worship.

2. *ʿĀlim al-ghayb* (the Knower of the unseen) is Allah ﷻ Alone. We are not allowed to attribute this quality to any creature whatsoever.

3. It is important that we confine the attribution of authority, specific to the Almighty, to Him alone, —for example, being the Creator, Omnipotent, Self-Reliant and Eternal and not in need of any other.

4. Only Allah ﷻ has the authority to accept invocations and supplications. Only He must be believed to have this.

5. There are certain actions that are specific to Allah ﷻ. He is Self-Sufficient in these matters and these actions belong to none other. The prime examples are creating the whole universe out of nothing and bringing it to an end, giving life and causing death, being worthy of worship, establishing Paradise and Hell, creating angels, assigning Prophets and Messengers with their prophethood and messengership, trusting them with revelation. Alternating day and night, keeping boats and ships safely afloat in deep oceans, sending winds and clouds etc.

6. There are certain beautiful names that cannot be given to anybody other than Him. He does not have any partner in them. Allah ﷻ alone must be invoked by the names that are attributed to Him by the Shariah. Calling upon others besides Him by those names is impermissible because it would be against the Shariah.

These are a few attributes that are confined to Almighty Allah.

Q.18. What is the difference between inherent attributes and given qualities?

Ans. Inherent attributes are the ones that are not given by somebody else. Nor is anybody else a cause of or means for them. Inherent attributes are confined to Allah سبحانه وتعالى Alone. None other than Him can have such attributes. On the other hand, bestowed qualities are always given by Allah سبحانه وتعالى with or without any apparent medium. These qualities belong to creation exclusively. [Attributing them to Allah سبحانه وتعالى would be an act of disbelief.] All the qualities of the Prophets fall within this category. They are given to them by Allah Almighty.

So, the difference between inherent and given attributes is that the former are confined to Allah سبحانه وتعالى whereas latter are confined to creation. It is an act of disbelief to attribute any of the latter to Allah سبحانه وتعالى whereas it is equally an act of disbelief to attribute any of the former to any other than Him.

Q.19. What does *Īmān bi al-Risāla* signify?

Ans. It means to believe that the prophethood of all the Prophets and messengership of all the Messengers—from Adam عليه السلام to our beloved Prophet Muhammad ﷺ—is the truth. All the Prophets were the most perfect example of truth raised by Allah سبحانه وتعالى during the times in which they were raised and worked to accomplish the same mission. They all worked under the same divine plan proposed by Allah سبحانه وتعالى.

Q.20. Who is a Messenger or a Prophet?

Ans. A Prophet or a Messenger is an individual through whom Allah ﷻ chooses to communicate His message to mankind and guide them rightly to the truth. Generally, both words have the same meaning. But, in more precise terms, every recipient of divine revelation is a prophet. A messenger is one who was also given a new law to call people to Allah ﷻ.[27]

Q.21. What is the difference between the messengership of our Prophet Muhammad ﷺ and the Prophets prior to him?

Ans. The Prophets and Messengers prior to our beloved Messenger Muhammad ﷺ were raised for certain nations, tribes and territories. Their messages were meant to respond to the demands of a particular set of circumstances. The messengership of our Prophet ﷺ, on the other hand, encompasses the whole of creation from Adam ﷺ to the end of time as declared by the Qurʾān:

قُلْ يَـٰٓأَيُّهَا ٱلنَّاسُ إِنِّى رَسُولُ ٱللَّهِ إِلَيْكُمْ جَمِيعًا.

> Say: O mankind! I have (come) to all of you (as) the Messenger of Allah.[28]

The noblest Prophet ﷺ said:

وَكَانَ النَّبِيُّ يُبْعَثُ إِلَى قَوْمِهِ خَاصَّةً، وَبُعِثْتُ إِلَى النَّاسِ كَافَّةً.

> Every prophet prior to me was sent to his own people but I have been raised for the whole of mankind.[29]

---

[27] al-Qasṭalānī, *al-Mawāhib al-laduniyya*, 2:47; and al-Zurqānī, *Sharḥ al-mawāhib al-laduniyya*, 4:86.
[28] Qurʾān 7:158.

Another hadith, which asserts that the Prophet ﷺ had been qualified as the final Prophet prior to the creation of Adam ؑ, explains it further. ʿIrbāḍ b. Sāriya ؓ said that the Holy Prophet ﷺ said:

إِنِّي عِنْدَ اللهِ فِي أُمِّ الْكِتَابِ لَخَاتَمُ النَّبِيِّيْنَ، وَإِنَّ آدَمَ لَمُنْجَدِلٌ فِيْ طِيْنَتِهِ.

> I had been (declared as) the final messenger in the *umm al-kitāb* while Adam ؑ was still unfermented clay.[30]

It clarifies that our Prophet Muhammad ﷺ was not only a Prophet but also the final Prophet prior to the preparation of clay to create Adam ؑ.

Q.22. What is the ruling regarding somebody who accepts any prophet whatsoever after our Prophet Muhammad ﷺ?

Ans. The noblest Prophet ﷺ was raised after all the Prophets. Prophethood was accomplished with him ﷺ and the chain of prophethood terminated with his prophethood. All of mankind till the Last Day will continue to benefit and draw blessings through his ﷺ spring of prophethood and there will never be another prophet. As it has been stated in the Holy Qurʾān:

مَّا كَانَ مُحَمَّدٌ أَبَآ أَحَدٍ مِّن رِّجَالِكُمْ وَلَٰكِن رَّسُولَ ٱللَّهِ وَخَاتَمَ ٱلنَّبِيِّـۧنَ ۗ وَكَانَ ٱللَّهُ بِكُلِّ شَيْءٍ عَلِيمًا.

> Muhammad ﷺ is not the father of any of your men, but he is the Messenger of Allah and the Last of the Prophets (ending the chain of the

---

[29] Narrated by al-Bukhārī in *al-Ṣaḥīḥ*, 1:128 §328.

[30] Narrated by Aḥmad b. Ḥanbal in *al-Musnad*, 4:128; and al-Ḥākim in *al-Mustadrak*, 2:656 §4175.

> Prophets). And Allah is the Perfect Knower of everything.[31]

All the exegetes of the Qur'ān, jurists, scholars of hadith, and all Imams—from as early as the companions of the Prophet ﷺ and the following generations until our times—unanimously declare the meaning of the expression *khātam al-nabiyyīn* as the last prophet. The same was said by the Holy Prophet ﷺ himself.

أَنَا خَاتَمُ النَّبِيِّيْنَ لَا نَبِيَّ بَعْدِيْ.

> I am the last Prophet and there is no Prophet whatsoever after me.[32]

This demonstrates that anybody who believes in any prophet whatsoever after our Prophet Muhammad ﷺ or finds such a prophet possible in any sense, is plainly and simply a non-believer.

Q.23. What is meant by *khātam al-nabiyyīn*?

Ans. It means that Allah ﷻ has completed and finalised the office of prophethood with our Prophet ﷺ. After the raising of our Prophet ﷺ, there is no more possibility of any other prophet whatsoever. Imam al-Tirmidhī narrates on the authority of Thawbān ؓ that the Prophet ﷺ said:

أَنَا خَاتَمُ النَّبِيِّيْنَ لَا نَبِيَّ بَعْدِيْ.

> I am the last Prophet and there is no Prophet whatsoever after me.[33]

So, the chain concludes with him ﷺ and anybody who proclaims prophethood or believes in such a person's

---

[31] Qur'ān 33:40.
[32] Narrated by al-Tirmidhī in *al-Sunan: Kitāb al-fitan* [The book of trials], 4:399 §2219.
[33] Ibid.

prophethood or believes that there could be a prophet in any sense after the proclamation of prophethood by our beloved Prophet ﷺ is a disbeliever—a rejecter of faith.

Q.24. What does *Īmān bi al-Ākhira* (faith in the Hereafter) mean?

Ans. It means to believe in life after death; that every person will be resurrected after death and will be held responsible and accountable in the court of Allah Almighty; that, consequently, he/she will be led to Paradise as a reward or dragged to Hellfire as punishment for his/her deeds. This life is known as the 'life Hereafter' (*al-ākhira*). Believing in that life is *īmān bi al-ākhira*.

Q.25. What is *al-Barzakh*?

Ans. A hindrance or a barrier between two things is known as *barzakh*. As a term of Shariah, it means the time span between a person's death and the Day of Resurrection. All humans and Jinns will stay in *barzakh* after they die according to their ranks. As the Qur'ān states:

> حَتَّىٰٓ إِذَا جَآءَ أَحَدَهُمُ ٱلْمَوْتُ قَالَ رَبِّ ٱرْجِعُونِ. لَعَلِّىٓ أَعْمَلُ صَٰلِحًا فِيمَا تَرَكْتُ ۚ كَلَّآ ۚ إِنَّهَا كَلِمَةٌ هُوَ قَآئِلُهَا ۖ وَمِن وَرَآئِهِم بَرْزَخٌ إِلَىٰ يَوْمِ يُبْعَثُونَ.
>
> Finally, when death comes to anyone of them, (then) he will say: 'O my Lord, send me back (to the world), So that I may do some righteous works in that (world) which I have left behind.' Not at all! He will be saying this (only in despair). And ahead of them is a barrier (erected)

> till the Day (when) they will be raised up (from the graves).[34]

The word rendered as 'barrier' has a twofold connection—with this world as well as with the Hereafter. The connection with this world means that if somebody among the departed's relations, friends, affiliates or acquaintance performs any righteous deeds —such as acts of charity, certain acts of worship, reciting Allah's names, etc.—to donate their rewards to the deceased one, it reaches him/her and brings peace and comfort. The connection with the Hereafter means that the comforts or torment earned by the dead in *barzakh* are actually their part in the Hereafter. Allah ﷻ says about Pharaoh and his people:

ٱلنَّارُ يُعْرَضُونَ عَلَيْهَا غُدُوًّا وَعَشِيًّا.

> They are brought before the Fire of Hell morning and evening.[35]

Q.26. What is *al-Qiyāma*?

Ans. It is the name for the day when Allah ﷻ will resurrect all the dead and hold them accountable for their good and bad deeds.

Q.27. What does *ʿAlāmāt al-Qiyāma* mean?

Ans. This means the signs of the Last Day. They will appear before the Day of Judgement. The appearance of Imam Mahdī ﵇, the decent of ʿĪsā (the Prophet Jesus) ﵇, the emergence of Gog and Magog and their perishing under the Divine Wrath, the Sunrise in the West and the appearance of a great fire are some of the main signs

---

[34] Qurʾān 23:99–100.
[35] Ibid., 40:46.

among many. In the end, the signs will appear, the angel Isrāfīl ﷺ will blow the trumpet at the command of Allah ﷻ and everything will perish. The trumpet will be blown again for as long as Allah ﷻ wills and this will bring all the dead back to life (the Resurrection).

Q.28. What is *Janna* (Paradise)?

Ans. It is the name for the abode of peace, relief and comfort which Allah ﷻ will grant the people of faith (the believers) as reward for their faith and righteous deeds.

Abū Hurayra ﷺ relates that Allah's Messenger ﷺ stated that Allah ﷻ declares:

> I have prepared something for my righteous servants, such a thing as no eye has seen (its beauty), no ear has heard (of its qualities) and no imagination has formed any idea of its reality. Its wall is made with alternate bricks of gold and silver and a cement of musk. Its land is made of Saffron, pearls and rubies instead of dust, pebbles and stones.[36]

The Holy Qur'ān states:

> كَأَنَّهُنَّ ٱلْيَاقُوتُ وَٱلْمَرْجَانُ.
>
> As if they (chaste maidens) were rubies and pearls.[37]
>
> وَزَرَابِيُّ مَبْثُوثَةٌ.
>
> And soft and refined carpets and rugs (richly) spread.[38]

---

[36] Narrated by al-Bukhārī in *al-Ṣaḥīḥ: Kitāb bad' al-khalq* [Beginning of Creation], 3:1185 §3072.

[37] Qur'ān 55:58.

[38] Ibid., 88:16.

In Paradise, there are 100 levels. Each is as wide as the distance from the earth to the sky. The span of doors is as wide as the distance a brisk horse will cover from in 70 years. The bounties therein are such that nobody can think or dream of. Its inhabitants will be receiving rich fruits, milk, honey, food and drink. Allah ﷻ says:

فِيهِمَا فَٰكِهَةٌ وَنَخْلٌ وَرُمَّانٌ.

> In them also there are fruits, date-palms and pomegranates.[39]

They will be adorned with such beauty that none could have dreamt of acquiring. It further states:

مُتَّكِـِٔينَ عَلَىٰ رَفْرَفٍ خُضْرٍ وَعَبْقَرِيٍّ حِسَانٍ.

> (The residents of Paradise) will be (sitting) reclining on cushions over green carpets and rare and exquisite fine rugs.[40]

Abū Hurayra and Abū Saʿīd al-Khudrī ﵄ narrate that the Prophet ﷺ declared that a herald will announce to the inhabitants of Paradise:

> 'You will remain healthy, never to become ill; live, never to die; stay young, never to age; enjoy comfort, never to toil in labour.'[41]

ʿAbd Allāh b. Umar ﵄ relates that Allah's Messenger ﷺ said:

> 'The person with the highest rank (in divine proximity) among the people of Paradise is the

---

[39] Ibid., 55:68.
[40] Ibid., 55:76.
[41] Narrated by Muslim in *al-Ṣaḥīḥ: Kitāb al-janna wa ṣifat naʿīmihā* [Paradise and its Characteristics], 4:2182 §2837.

one who will be honoured with the beatific vision of the divine countenance day in, day out.'

Then the Prophet ﷺ recited the following verse of the Qur'ān:

وُجُوهٌ يَوْمَئِذٍ نَّاضِرَةٌ. إِلَىٰ رَبِّهَا نَاظِرَةٌ.

Many faces will be fresh and in full bloom that Day, Viewing (the enchanting radiance and beauty of) their Lord (unveiled).[42]

Q.29. What is Hell?

Ans. It is the name for the abode prepared for evildoers and disbelievers and they will be hurled there after the reckoning on the Day of Judgement. The disbelievers will be condemned there for eternity. It holds dark blazing fire bursting forth without the slightest flare of light. Allah ﷻ says:

إِنَّ ٱللَّهَ لَعَنَ ٱلْكَٰفِرِينَ وَأَعَدَّ لَهُمْ سَعِيرًا. خَٰلِدِينَ فِيهَآ أَبَدًا ۖ لَّا يَجِدُونَ وَلِيًّا وَلَا نَصِيرًا.

Surely Allah has cursed the disbelievers and has kept ready for them the Blazing Fire (of Hell). They will live in it forever. They will find neither any caring friend nor any supporting helper.[43]

At another place, the Holy Qur'ān states:

وَمَن يَعْصِ ٱللَّهَ وَرَسُولَهُۥ فَإِنَّ لَهُۥ نَارَ جَهَنَّمَ خَٰلِدِينَ فِيهَآ أَبَدًا.

---

[42] Qur'ān 75:23.

[43] Ibid., 33:64–65.

> And whoever disobeys Allah and His Messenger ﷺ, surely there is for him the Fire of Hell in which they will live forever.[44]

Q.30. What does *Īmān bi al-kutub* mean?

Ans. There have been a great number of Prophets and Messengers from Adam ﷺ to our beloved Prophet Muhammad ﷺ. Among them, there were some whom Allah ﷻ chose to reveal His message in the form of Divine Books and Heavenly Scriptures. To believe in all those scriptures as being from Allah ﷻ is *īmān bi al-kutub*.

Q.31. What are the Heavenly Books known to us and who are the corresponding Messengers to whom each was revealed?

Ans. Allah ﷻ has revealed numerous scriptures and books for the guidance of different peoples. The following four are known to mankind along with the Messengers to whom they were revealed.

1. Torah (The Old Testament): Prophet Mūsā [Moses] ﷺ
2. Zabūr (Psalms): Prophet Dāwūd [David] ﷺ
3. Injīl (The New Testament/Holy Bible): Prophet ʿĪsā [Jesus] ﷺ
4. Qurʾān: The last and the most comprehensively inclusive book revealed to the Beloved of Allah, Muhammad ﷺ.

---

[44] Ibid., 72:23.

Q.32. Are the Heavenly Books prior to the Holy Qur'ān still in their original form?

Ans. No. None of these Heavenly Books except for the Holy Qur'ān is in its original form. The people who received those books from their Prophets changed the divine commandments communicated to them of their own accord. The Qur'ān, on the other hand, is unique in this respect. It is still in its original form. Allah ﷻ Himself has taken the responsibility of keeping it safe from human hands. It says:

إِنَّا نَحْنُ نَزَّلْنَا ٱلذِّكْرَ وَإِنَّا لَهُۥ لَحَٰفِظُونَ.

> Assuredly We alone have revealed this Glorious Admonition (the Qur'ān), and surely We alone will guard it.[45]

So, the Qur'ān is the only divine book which holds the most complete code of life and the most perfect guidance for mankind till the last day.

Q.33. What are the rulings regarding previous Heavenly Books after the revelation of the Qur'ān?

Ans. After the revelation of the Qur'ān, it is still essential to believe in all the previous books as being from Allah ﷻ. We must also know that it is no longer obligatory to follow the commandments that they carry. The reason for this is simply that none of the books prior to the Qur'ān claims to be a universal Heavenly Book meant to guide all of mankind. All of them were rather for the guidance of particular communities. For this reason, people prior to the revelation of the Qur'ān, had fallen victim to severe differences of opinion regarding following this book or

---

[45] Ibid., 15:9.

that; each group claimed the truthfulness of the set of religious beliefs and rituals to which they adhered. It was a natural demand of the time that one book of ultimate guidance should be revealed, a book which could invite all factions of mankind to unity under the banner of humanity and upon a single platform. This is why the Qurʾān says:

إِنْ هُوَ إِلَّا ذِكْرٌ لِّلْعَٰلَمِينَ.

This Qurʾān is but a reminder to all mankind.[46]

That is why the Qurʾān came as a matchless source of guidance for the whole of mankind till the Last Day.

Q.34. What does *Īmān bi al-Malāʾika* [Belief in Angels] mean?

Ans. The word *al-malāʾika* (angel) comes from *al-malak*. It is pluralised as *al-malāʾik* and *al-malāʾika*. The origin literally means 'to own; to be angel; ownership or power, control and authority'. It also refers to the power of control over a matter. The word *al-malāʾika* is also used for Heavenly Souls.[47]

They are called *al-malāʾika* because Allah ﷻ assigns different matters to them, giving them power and authority to carry these out. They also perform the duty of communicating Allah's messages to His chosen individuals. They are subtle creatures of light. Human beings, generally, cannot see them. Some people deny the physical existence of angels—foolishly—because they lack good enough appreciation of the matter. They rather interpret the Qurʾānic mention of angels as abstract forces, which is sheer misguidance. Angels are dignified

---

[46] Ibid., 12:104.

[47] Rāghib al-Aṣfahānī, *al-Mufradāt*, pp. 472–473.

creatures that carry out divine commands. To believe in their existence and all related details is termed *īmān bi al-malā'ika*.

Q.35. Who are the angels and what are they made of?

Ans. Angels are Allah's creation of light. It is wrong to believe that they are human spirits or divine attributes or forces of good or evil. In the academic, philosophical and theological history of humanity, there have been a number of opinions about the reality of angels. The notion held by the majority of Muslim scholars is stated as follows:

فَذَهَبَ أَكْثَرُ الْمُسْلِمِيْنَ إِلَى أَنَّهَا أَجْسَامٌ لَطِيْفَةٌ، قَادِرَةٌ عَلَى التَّشَكُّلِ بِأَشْكَالٍ مُخْتَلِفَةٍ.

According to the majority of Muslims, they are entities made of light capable of adopting different shapes.[48]

'Ā'isha ﵁ reports that the Prophet ﷺ said,

خُلِقَتِ الْمَلَائِكَةُ مِنْ نُوْرٍ، وَخُلِقَ الْجَانُّ مِنْ مَّارِجٍ مِنْ نَّارٍ، وَخُلِقَ آدَمُ مِمَّا وُصِفَ لَكُمْ.

The angels are created with light, Jinn are created with blazing fire and human are created with what has been described for you (dust).[49]

---

[48] Al-Bayḍāwī, *al-Tafsīr*, 1:80–81.

[49] Narrated by Muslim in *al-Ṣaḥīḥ: Kitāb al-Zuhd* [The Book of Piety], 4:2294 §2996; Aḥmad b. Ḥanbal in *al-Musnad*, 6:153 and 168; and Ibn Ḥibbān in *al-Ṣaḥīḥ*, 14:25 §6155.

Q.36. WHAT ARE THE DUTIES AND RESPONSIBILITIES OF ANGELS?

ANS. Unquestioning obedience is a distinctive characteristic of angels. They discharge different duties according to divine command. The power they have is not their own. Allah ﷻ said:

يَخَافُونَ رَبَّهُم مِّن فَوْقِهِمْ وَيَفْعَلُونَ مَا يُؤْمَرُونَ.

They continue to fear their Lord, Who is high above them, and obey whatever the command they are given.[50]

Ibn Sābiṭ ؓ says that all that will happen till the Day of Judgement has been already written in *umm al-kitāb* (the secure tablet). Three angels have been appointed to supervise it. Gabriel ؑ has been given the books to communicate it to His Messengers. The matters of afflicting Divine wrath have also been submitted to him. When Allah ﷻ decides a community's annihilation, He appoints Gabriel to help (His friends) against His enemies. The matters pertaining to security, rains and greenery have been submitted to Mīkā'īl ؑ. The matter of withdrawing souls from bodies (causing death) has been submitted to the Angel of Death. When this world ends, the records of human beings' deeds will be collected and compared against the *umm al-kitāb*. These regulators (of all matters—angels) will find them in complete agreement with it.'[51]

Abū Hurayra ؓ narrates that the Prophet ﷺ said:

---

[50] Qur'ān 16:50.
[51] Narrated by Ibn Ḥibbān in *al-ʿAẓama*, 3:973 §496.

إِنَّ طَرَفَ صَاحِبِ الصُّوْرِ مُذْ وُكِّلَ بِهِ مُسْتَعِدٌّ، يَنْظُرُ نَحْوَ الْعَرْشِ مَخَافَةَ أَنْ يُؤْمَرَ قَبْلَ أَنْ يَرْتَدَّ إِلَيْهِ طَرَفُهُ، كَأَنَّ عَيْنَيْهِ كَوْكَبَانِ دُرِّيَّانِ.

There is no doubt that Isrāfīl, ever since he has been appointed to blow the trumpet, is ever ready with his eyes upon the Throne without a blink lest he should be directed (to blow it) before blinking his eyes. As if his both eyes are shining stars.[52]

Q.37. Who are the angels who keep the record of human deeds?

Ans. They are known as *kirāman kātibīn*. The Holy Qur'ān states:

وَإِنَّ عَلَيْكُمْ لَحَـٰفِظِينَ. كِرَامًا كَـٰتِبِينَ. يَعْلَمُونَ مَا تَفْعَلُونَ.

Whereas there are guardian angels appointed over you, (Who are) dignified, the scribes (writing the records of all your deeds). They know (all) those (actions) which you do.[53]

Likewise, we find at another place in the Holy Qur'ān:

أَمْ أَبْرَمُوٓا۟ أَمْرًا فَإِنَّا مُبْرِمُونَ. أَمْ يَحْسَبُونَ أَنَّا لَا نَسْمَعُ سِرَّهُمْ وَنَجْوَىٰهُم ۚ بَلَىٰ وَرُسُلُنَا لَدَيْهِمْ يَكْتُبُونَ.

Have they (the disbelievers of Makka) finalized (any scheme against the Messenger ﷺ)? So We (too) are going to take the ultimate decision. Do they think that We do not hear their secret talk and whisperings? Why not? (We do listen.) And

[52] Narrated by al-Ḥākim in *al-Mustadrak*, 4:603 §8676.

[53] Qur'ān 82:10–12.

> the angels sent by Us also remain with them busy writing.[54]

Ibn Jurayj states:

> *Kirāman kātibīn* are two angels. One stays on a human's right side and keeps recording righteous deeds. The other one stays on the left side and keeps recording evil deeds.

The one on the right side records the righteous deeds without asking the one on the left to witness whereas the one on the left side does not write any evil deed without asking the one on the right side to witness it. They stay on the right and left sides when the person under their supervision sits; one is ahead of him and the other behind him when he walks; one towards his head and the other towards his feet when he sleeps.[55]

The Qur'ān states:

> إِذْ يَتَلَقَّى ٱلْمُتَلَقِّيَانِ عَنِ ٱلْيَمِينِ وَعَنِ ٱلشِّمَالِ قَعِيدٌ. مَّا يَلْفِظُ مِن قَوْلٍ إِلَّا لَدَيْهِ رَقِيبٌ عَتِيدٌ.

> When the two receivers receive (the recording angels write down his every communication and work), sitting on the right and on the left, Not a word does he utter with the mouth but a watcher is there beside him ready (to write it).[56]

Q.38. What does *Īmān bi al-Qadr* mean?

Ans. Allah ﷻ has eternally known all the conditions, states, circumstances and situations through which any

---

[54] Qur'ān 43:79–80.

[55] Narrated Ibn Ḥibbān in *al-ʿAẓama*, 3:1000 §519.

[56] Qur'ān 50:17–18.

individual passes during his life in this world. He has written it down on the *al-lawḥ al-maḥfūẓ*—the secure tablet. He has created both the good and the evil regarding each individual's personal life and endowed him with the freedom of choice as to which of the two paths—good or evil—he adopts for himself. Allah ﷻ mentions so in the Qur'ān:

أَلَمْ نَجْعَل لَّهُۥ عَيْنَيْنِ. وَلِسَانًا وَشَفَتَيْنِ. وَهَدَيْنَٰهُ ٱلنَّجْدَيْنِ.

> Have We not made for him two eyes? And (have We not given him) a tongue and two lips? And (have We also not) shown him the two highways (of good and evil)?[57]

This explains that human beings are not merely helpless, incapable of doing anything of their own accord. The truth of the matter is that whatever human hands have earned or are going to earn is all a part of Divine Knowledge. This is known as *al-qadr* (destiny). Believing in it the way we have just mentioned is faith in destiny [*īmān bi al-qadr*].

Q.39. What do *Qaḍā* and *Qadr* mean?

Ans. The word *qaḍā* literally means to judge (judicially), to execute (a command) or to perform (a duty). Allah ﷻ has created this great manifest of divine power and control (our universe—the whole of creation) and subjected it to certain laws, which are called the laws of nature. These laws work to execute the divine decree and He creates new creatures whenever appropriate and wherever suitable according to His will. This word refers to the laws of nature—such as the law of cause and effect.

---

[57] Ibid., 90:8–10.

For example, it has been decreed that good deeds will bear good fruits whereas evil deeds will bring evil ends. Allah ﷻ says:

$$\text{لَهَا مَا كَسَبَتْ وَعَلَيْهَا مَا اكْتَسَبَتْ.}$$

There is a reward for whatever good it has earned and there is torment for whatever evil it has perpetrated.[58]

Qadr literally means to estimate, to ordain or to decree.[59]

Allah ﷻ eternally knows every single creature's deeds, conditions and states. The word *qadr* refers to the part of that knowledge which has been transferred to the *al-lawḥ al-maḥfūẓ* (the secure tablet). Allah ﷻ says:

$$\text{وَكُلَّ شَيْءٍ أَحْصَيْنَاهُ فِي إِمَامٍ مُّبِينٍ.}$$

And We have encompassed everything in the illumining Book (*al-lawḥ al-maḥfūẓ*).[60]

ʿAbd Allāh b. ʿAmr ؓ narrates that the Master of the creation ﷺ said: 'Allah ﷻ had written the destiny of all the creation fifty thousand years prior to the creation of the Earth and the Heavens (this physical Universe) while His Throne was upon water.'[61]

---

[58] Ibid., 2:286.
[59] Rāghib al-Aṣfahānī, *al-Mufradāt*, p. 395.
[60] Qurʾān 36:12.
[61] Narrated by Muslim in *al-Ṣaḥīḥ: Kitāb al-qadr* [Book of Destiny], 4:2044 §2653.

Q.40. Is the destiny written on *al-Lawḥ al-Maḥfūẓ* final or is it subject to possible changes?

Ans. No. It is not an absolute final decision. Destiny, as a matter of fact, is of three types:

1. *Mubram ḥaqīqī* (Irrevocable/permanent)
2. *Mubram ghayr ḥaqīqī* (Semi-irrevocable—cannot be withdrawn or held back except by certain means)
3. *Muʿallaq* (Revocable)

The first type represents the final decision. It cannot be changed at all. For example, when the angels were sent down to the people of Lūṭ [Lot] ﷺ to execute the commandment of inflicting divine torment upon them, Ibrāhīm [Abraham] ﷺ requested Allah ﷻ to cancel it. Allah ﷻ said to Ibrāhīm ﷺ:

يَٰٓإِبْرَٰهِيمُ أَعْرِضْ عَنْ هَٰذَآ إِنَّهُۥ قَدْ جَآءَ أَمْرُ رَبِّكَ وَإِنَّهُمْ ءَاتِيهِمْ عَذَابٌ غَيْرُ مَرْدُودٍ.

(The angels said:) 'O Ibrāhīm (Abraham)! Leave off this (matter). Surely the Command of (torment from) your Lord has now come to pass, and the torment is about to seize them which cannot be averted.'[62]

The only reason for that was that it was a destiny that could not be withdrawn.

The second type—that is, the semi-irrevocable—is irrevocable but the strength is not such that no appropriate source (among those that Allah ﷻ has created) could possibly intervene. Thus it could be reversed or withdrawn or changed. This is the type about which al-Shaykh ʿAbd al-Qādir al-Jīlānī has said that he

---

[62] Qurʾān 11:76.

can reverse the irreversible destiny. The word of the Holy Prophet ﷺ about such destiny says:

لَا يَرُدُّ الْقَضَاءَ إِلَّا الدُّعَاءُ.

> Only supplication can reverse the destiny.[63]

إِنَّ الدُّعَاءَ يَرُدُّ الْقَضَاءَ الْمُبْرَمَ.

> Undoubtedly, supplication can reverse the semi-irrevocable destiny.[64]

The third and last is *muʿallaq* destiny, which is within the reach of many saintly friends of Allah and other righteous people. It could be changed through any of Allah's blessings, such as the prophetic intercession, supplications of honourable friends of Allah ﷻ, serving your parents and performing charitable acts. Allah ﷻ has promised that He changes the destiny of a sincere and chosen servant in tandem with his changing intention and supplication, if He wishes so. It says in the Qurʾān:

يَمْحُوا۟ ٱللَّهُ مَا يَشَآءُ وَيُثْبِتُ وَعِندَهُۥٓ أُمُّ ٱلْكِتَٰبِ.

> Allah erases whatever (writing) He wills and confirms (whatever He wills). And with Him alone is the Real Book (the Protected Tablet [*al-lawḥ al-maḥfūẓ*]).[65]

Iblīs did not show respect for Adam ﷺ by prostrating to him and this made him a disbeliever. That accursed one said:

---

[63] Narrated by al-Tirmidhī in *al-Ṣaḥīḥ: Kitāb al-qadr* (Book of Destiny), 4:448 §2139.

[64] Narrated by al-Daylamī in *al-Firdaws bi-māthūr al-khiṭāb*, 5:364 §8448.

[65] Qurʾān 13:39.

قَالَ رَبِّ فَأَنظِرْنِيٓ إِلَىٰ يَوْمِ يُبْعَثُونَ. قَالَ فَإِنَّكَ مِنَ ٱلْمُنظَرِينَ. إِلَىٰ يَوْمِ ٱلْوَقْتِ ٱلْمَعْلُومِ.

He said: 'O Lord, then grant me respite till the Day (when) people will be raised up (again).' Allah said: 'So, indeed, you are among those granted respite, Till the Day of the appointed time (resurrection).'[66]

If Allah ﷻ can accept the supplication of Satan the cursed one and change his destiny (give him life until the Last Day), He can most certainly change the destiny through the supplications of His true friends.

During the time of ʿUmar ؓ, the second rightly-guided caliph, a plague broke out in Syria, while he travelled there. To escape the spread of the epidemic, he hastened to leave the area. Abū ʿUbayda ؓ said:

أَتَفِرُّ مِنْ قَدَرِ اللهِ؟.

Do you escape from the destiny of Allah?

He replied:

أَفِرُّ مِنْ قَضَاءِ اللهِ إِلَى قَدَرِ اللهِ.

I escape from the rule of (nature set by) Allah (such as cause and effect in this case) towards the destiny of Allah.[67]

This means: 'if there is an epidemic and I manage to save myself from it by escaping to some other place, my prevention of exposure to that illness would be Allah's destiny (what Allah ﷻ has written on the basis of His prior knowledge of it).'

---

[66] Ibid., 15:36–38.

[67] Narrated by Ibn Saʿd in *al-Ṭabaqāt al-kubrā*, 3:283.

The above-mentioned verse and hadith explain that Allah ﷻ changes the writing of the protected tablet as He pleases, from His prior knowledge. Such a change happens in the form of revocable destiny.

Q.41. ARE WE ALLOWED TO CONSIDER THE ISSUE OF DESTINY?

ANS.No. We are not allowed to reflect upon it because we cannot grasp it. The hadith of the Prophet ﷺ directs us not to contemplate the issue of divine destiny for it can potentially lead to the destruction of faith.

عَنْ أَبِي هُرَيْرَةَ ﵁ قَالَ خَرَجَ عَلَيْنَا رَسُوْلُ اللهِ ﷺ وَنَحْنُ نَتَنَازَعُ فِي الْقَدَرِ، فَغَضِبَ حَتَّى احْمَرَّ وَجْهُهُ، حَتَّى كَأَنَّمَا فُقِيَ فِي وَجْنَتَيْهِ حَبُّ الرُّمَّانِ، فَقَالَ: أَبِهَذَا أُمِرْتُمْ أَمْ بِهَذَا أُرْسِلْتُ إِلَيْكُمْ؟ إِنَّمَا هَلَكَ مَنْ كَانَ قَبْلَكُمْ حِيْنَ تَنَازَعُوْا فِي هَذَا الْأَمْرِ، عَزَمْتُ عَلَيْكُمْ أَنْ لَّا تَنَازَعُوْا فِيْهِ.

Abu Hurayra ﷺ narrates that Allah's Messenger ﷺ came out to us while we were discussing the matter of destiny (and were at variance upon it). The indignation reddened his face as if the grains of pomegranate had been squeezed upon his holy cheeks. Then he ﷺ said, 'Have you been commanded of this? Have I been sent to you with this? The communities prior to you were destroyed when they disputed about this issue. I adjure you never to discuss this matter.'

Q.42. WHAT IS MEANT BY THE DĪN OF ISLAM'?

ANS. Dīn of Islam stands for an all-embracing and perfectly comprehensive code of life based on the commandments of Allah ﷻ and His Messenger ﷺ that fulfils all the needs of every sphere of human life. It includes guidance for every aspect of human life from the individual to the national to the international level. The Holy Qur'ān states:

إِنَّ ٱلدِّينَ عِندَ ٱللَّهِ ٱلْإِسْلَٰمُ.

> Truly, Islam is the only *dīn* (Religion) in Allah's sight.[68]

It also states:

ٱلْيَوْمَ أَكْمَلْتُ لَكُمْ دِينَكُمْ وَأَتْمَمْتُ عَلَيْكُمْ نِعْمَتِي وَرَضِيتُ لَكُمُ ٱلْإِسْلَٰمَ دِينًا.

> Today I have perfected your *dīn* (Religion) for you, and have completed My Blessing upon you, and have chosen for you Islam (as) *dīn* (a complete code of life).[69]

The concept of Islam as a complete and perfect code of life (*dīn*) emanates from these verses.

Q.43. What is the difference between *Īmān* and Islam?

Ans. Islam and *īmān* are, as a matter of fact, two sides of the same coin. The principal, simple difference is that what *īmān* requires us to believe in the heart and confirm with the tongue, Islam requires us to verify through our practice. In other words, *īmān* means to believe in the requisites of faith, to be true at heart and to assert them

[68] Qur'ān 3:19.
[69] Ibid., 5:3.

by the tongue, while Islam means to submit, obey and act accordingly.[70]

Q.44. What does it mean to be a Muslim?

Ans. Being a Muslim means to follow Islam as the *dīn*. According to the Prophet ﷺ, a Muslim is the only person who can be a source of peace and security and a fountainhead of welfare and prosperity. A hadith asserts:

> A Muslim is a person from whose hand and tongue (action and word), other Muslims' honour, wealth and soul are safe [i.e., a person who does not harm any other person's honour, property or life through word or action].

Q.45. What is the basic condition for becoming a Muslim?

Ans. The basic condition for becoming Muslim is to declare it by the tongue. It means to recite *al-shahāda* and announce that one has accepted Islam and is a Muslim now so that other people may consider him/her a Muslim and behave towards him/her as a Muslim. It will also enable him/her to enjoy the rights to which he/she is entitled as a Muslim.

Q.46. What is the al-shahāda?

Ans. It is *lā ilāha ill-Allāhu Muḥammad'ur rasūl Allāh*—لَا إِلَٰهَ إِلَّا اللهُ مُحَمَّدٌ رَّسُوْلُ اللهِ—(There is none worthy of worship but Allah and Muhammad ﷺ is Allah's Messenger). This is known as *al-kalima al-ṭayyiba*.

---

[70] For a detailed discussion on the topic, see Shaykh-ul-Islam Dr Muhammad Tahir-ul-Qadri's *Fatwa on Terrorism and Suicide Bombings*.

Q.47. Can a person become a Muslim if he/she says *al-Shahāda* in his/her own language?

Ans. Yes, if someone confirms the acceptance of Allah's unity and the Holy Prophet Muhammad's ﷺ messengership in his/her own language, he/she thereby becomes a Muslim.

Q.48. Is there any other *al-Shahāda* other than *al-kalima al-ṭayyiba* whereby one becomes Muslim by reciting it?

Ans. Yes, it is called *kalima shahāda*. It runs as follows:

أَشْهَدُ أَنْ لَّا إِلَهَ إِلَّا اللهُ وَأَشْهَدُ أَنَّ مُحَمَّداً عَبْدُهُ وَرَسُوْلُهُ.

> I bear witness that there is none worthy of worship but Allah and I bear witness that Muhammad ﷺ is His servant and Messenger.

Q.49. What is the difference between *al-kalima al-ṭayyiba* and *kalima shahāda*?

Ans. The difference between the two is that *al-kalima al-ṭayyiba* contains only the expression of God's Unity and Muhammad's ﷺ messengership. *Kalima shahāda*, on the other hand, expresses God's Unity and Muhammad's ﷺ messengership in the form of bearing witness to them.

Q.50. How can we confirm the acceptance of Islam by a dumb person?

Ans. It would be enough for a dumb person to express through the signs that he/she normally uses to communicate—or in proper sign language in case he/she knows it—that there is no God but Allah, Muhammad ﷺ is His last prophet and whatever Islam says is the final truth.

Q.51. What is the ruling regarding one who denies one of the requisites of the *Dīn*?

Ans. Whoever denies the truth of any one of the requisites of the *dīn*—such as God's Unity, Messengership, the Day of Resurrection, angels, Paradise, Hellfire or Heavenly Books—is out of the ambit of Islam.

Q.52. Why is our faith weak despite our being Muslims?

Ans. The main reason that our *īmān* is weak is the intrusion of hypocrisy, jealousy and theological differences into our behaviour. These have been constantly causing corruption and deficiencies in our practice as well as weakening our moral standards. The situation has deteriorated to such an extent that we ignore Allah and His Messenger's pleasure just out of expediency and for the sake of personal worldly gain. We actually worship the lusts of our lower self and aim for worldly convenience. If we stand at a fork in the road where one path leads to guidance and the other to false tradition and evil convention, we don't think twice before following the latter. Our faces manifest a great deal of renunciation, piety, abstinence and righteousness; yet, at the same time, we may not find a greater liar, or one more deceitful and hypocritical, if we dared to look behind that mask. Our *īmān* is weak despite being Muslim because of such two-faced behaviour and double standards.

Q.53. How can we attain the state of strong faith?

Ans. We can regain the state of strong *īmān* if we habituate ourselves to keeping a watchful eye upon ourselves; holding ourselves accountable constantly; not just confining ourselves to invoking the name of Islam but practising it; and leading the life of true believers by following the Qur'ān and the Sunna as a model of perfection—as it is before our eyes in the form of the *sīra* (biography) of our beloved Prophet ﷺ.

Q.54. How many levels of certainty are there?

Ans. Certainty has three levels, namely:

1. *ʿIlm* (علم)—knowledge
2. *ʿIrfān* (عرفان)—cognition or perfect knowledge
3. *Īqān* (إيقان)—strong conviction

The *Sufis* term them as *ʿilm al-yaqīn* (علم اليقين), *ʿayn al-yaqīn* (عين اليقين) and *ḥaqq al-yaqīn* (حق اليقين).

Q.55. What does *ʿilm al-yaqīn* mean?

Ans. It is the first level of *īmān* which is termed as *al-īmān bi'l-ghayb* (faith in the unseen) and *ʿilm al-yaqīn* (the knowledge of certainty). Allah ﷻ declares:

ٱلَّذِينَ يُؤْمِنُونَ بِٱلْغَيْبِ.

Those who believe in the unseen.[71]

Those who believe in the unseen, evidence of which has reached them through a truthful being who has observed reality unveiled. So, the first requirement of faith is to believe in Allah and all other hidden and invisible realities based only on the fact that they have reached us through the truthful informant who has observed the divine countenance. In other words, faith in the unseen means to believe in whatever the Holy Prophet ﷺ has said without losing or doubting a single word of it. An analogy to explain the matter might be helpful. A

---

[71] Ibid., 2:3.

person gives his word that he has witnessed the murder of Mr A at such and such place by Mr B. To believe his word, without seeing the incident ourselves, because we trust in his truthfulness, is the first level of faith in the unseen. Belief in Allah without seeing Him, like this, is 'belief in unseen'.

Q.56. What does ʿ*irfān* (cognition) mean?

Ans. Then we reach the second level of *īmān* which is called ʿ*irfān* (cognition). On this level, we strengthen our faith by collecting the credible evidence to stand witness for the reality in which we believe. This could be termed 'cognition through evident signs'. The Holy Qurʾān mentions it in these words:

وَفِى ٱلْأَرْضِ ءَايَٰتٌ لِّلْمُوقِنِينَ. وَفِىٓ أَنفُسِكُمْ ۚ أَفَلَا تُبْصِرُونَ.

> And there are many Signs in the earth for the people with the truth of certitude (i.e., people of perfect certitude), and in your selves (as well). So do you not notice?[72]

This verse reminds us that the ability and capacity to derive correct conclusions by reflecting on Allah's endless power and limitless authority and believing in His perfection are all there within ourselves. All the facts that reveal His authority and their signs are within us too. All we need to do is to look into ourselves, to lift the dark veils of our humanity in an attempt to comprehend reality. We shall see how the realities glisten to us from within.

A close analogy to grasp the point could be that of a person, agitated and disturbed, who comes out of a building with a bloody knife in his hand and his clothes

---

[72] Ibid., 51:21.

covered with blood, and shoots off. If somebody were to perceive this situation, which is an evident sign of the occurrence of a gruesome crime, and believes that a murder has been committed, it would be cognition—the second level of *īmān*.

Q.57. What is *Īqān*?

Ans. The third level of *īmān* is known as *īqān* (strong conviction). The Holy Qur'ān has recorded the following about Ibrāhīm ﷺ:

وَإِذْ قَالَ إِبْرَاهِيْمُ رَبِّ أَرِنِي كَيْفَ تُحْيِ الْمَوْتَىٰ.

> And (also recall the event) when Ibrāhīm (Abraham) said: 'My Lord, show me how You bring the dead to life.'[73]

Here, we ask ourselves a question, 'Did not Ibrāhīm ﷺ know prior to this question that Allah ﷻ has power to bring dead to life?' The answer is definitely 'Yes! He did.' The wisdom behind recording this conversation is that the Qur'ān wants *us* to understand that the *īmān* of Ibrāhīm ﷺ was at the level of *ʿirfān*. This request to view the process with his eyes was for raising it to the third level through 'strong conviction by observation (*īqān bi'l-mushahada*)'. The conversation goes further:

قَالَ أَوَلَمْ تُؤْمِن.

> Allah said: 'Do you not have faith?'

The reply naturally is:

قَالَ بَلَىٰ وَلَٰكِن لِّيَطْمَئِنَّ قَلْبِي.

[73] Ibid., 2:260.

> He submitted: 'Why not! (I do believe,) but (I wish) my heart is blessed with gratifying calm.'

Allah ﷻ knew why Ibrāhīm ﷺ had made his request but the conversation was to teach us. It goes on:

> قَالَ فَخُذْ أَرْبَعَةً مِّنَ ٱلطَّيْرِ فَصُرْهُنَّ إِلَيْكَ ثُمَّ ٱجْعَلْ عَلَىٰ كُلِّ جَبَلٍ مِّنْهُنَّ جُزْءًا ثُمَّ ٱدْعُهُنَّ يَأْتِينَكَ سَعْيًا ۚ وَٱعْلَمْ أَنَّ ٱللَّهَ عَزِيزٌ حَكِيمٌ.
>
> Allah ordained: 'Well, take four birds and tame them to feel attached to you; then (slaughter them and) place a piece of each of them on each hill; then call them. They will come to you at high speed. And know that surely Allah is All-Mighty, All-Wise[74]

That is exactly what this verse shows us. Ibrāhīm ﷺ had obtained faith at the level of knowledge and developed it to the level of cognition. Now he wanted to move further to the level of *ḥaqq al-yaqīn* through visual experience. That is what Allah ﷻ granted him. The purpose of showing Ibrāhīm ﷺ, practically, the signs of divine power of disposal, was to improve the grade of his *īmān* to the level of *īqān* (إيقان) which is the highest level of *īmān*.

In order to appreciate the difference we can go through the analogy of two persons each of whom has blood on his clothes as well as on the knife he has in his hand; one has just slaughtered an animal whereas the other is fleeing a crime scene where he has committed the grave crime of killing a human being. Now, those who had not witnessed their actions would certainly be confused as to which was guilty of the crime. Suppose we had somebody who had literally witnessed both actions in

[74] Ibid., 2:260.

process. He would undoubtedly recognise the killer. Such a person is the person with *īqān*.

Q.58. What are the lowest and the highest levels of *īmān*?

Ans. The hadith of Gabriel explains the point delicately under the caption of *iḥsān*. When Gabriel asked what *iḥsān* is, the Prophet ﷺ said:

أَنْ تَعْبُدَ اللهَ كَأَنَّكَ تَرَاهُ، فَإِنْ لَّمْ تَكُنْ تَرَاهُ فَإِنَّهُ يَرَاكَ.

> The highest level of *īmān*—*iḥsān*—means that you worship Allah ﷻ as if you observe Him. If you don't see Him, (then the least of the *īmān* is that you be certain of the fact that) He observes you.[75]

It would be a gross mistake to assume that the application of the word 'worship' in this hadith—which stands here for the objective of human life—is confined to what is normally categorised as rituals such as Ṣalāh, Zakat, Ṣawm, etc. The Qur'ānic concept of worship and the Islamic concept of righteousness are, in fact, so vast and comprehensive that they cover all intellectual as well as practical aspects of human life. The Islamic understanding of worship wants to see human life embody all of the following qualities:

1. Sound faith: Human faith must be correct. This includes correct faith in Allah, the Hereafter, angels, the Heavenly Books and the Prophets.
2. Love of Allah: One must have a profound love for Allah ﷻ, the proof of which should appear in the form of

---

[75] Narrated by al-Bukhārī in *al-Ṣaḥīḥ: Kitāb al-īmān* [Book of Faith], chapter: 'On the Questioning of Gabriel', 1:27 §50.

helping our fellow human beings and in financial sacrifice for their welfare.

3. ALTRUISM: Allah ﷻ has granted man provisions and control over sources of wealth and its production. He requires of us to spend on our deserving blood relatives, orphans, the penniless, indigents, the needy and those chained by slavery and oppression so that mankind enjoys true freedom with economic rehabilitation and prosperity.

4. SOUND DEEDS: We must firmly abide by the rulings of Shariah and the 5 pillars of Islam.

5. KEEPING OUR WORD: It is important that we keep our word, fulfil our promises and remain resolute in whatever good we plan to do.

6. PATIENCE AND FORBEARING: One must not lose heart or lose endurance and perseverance in harsh and turbulent circumstances. One must, instead, see through oppressive situations with courage and dignity.

7. JIHAD: One must never be apprehensive or afraid in the face of opposition and hostility while working under the banner of truth and defending the right against the wrong, even if the evil resistance of falsehood against truth and right manages to engage him in open warfare.

The above-mentioned qualities are the essential elements of the *Dīn*. 'Righteousness and worship' indeed is a balanced combination of them all. So, worship at its root is a totality and all religious and secular matters are its constituent elements. If we detach any portion of human life, which is worship in all its aspects, it can't be declared as worship accomplished. A totality cannot be declared a totality if one or more of its elements is detached.

This brief discussion has brought us to the conclusion that the highest level of *īmān* would be a life in a state of constant observance of the divine countenance. The lowest level, on the other hand, would be a life in a constant state of certainty that Allah ﷻ sees me as it suits Him.

There is another hadith that explains these levels of faith from a different perspective. The Holy Prophet ﷺ said:

مَنْ رَأَى مِنْكُمْ مُنْكَراً فَلْيُغَيِّرْهُ بِيَدِهِ، فَإِنْ لَمْ يَسْتَطِعْ فَبِلِسَانِهِ، فَإِنْ لَمْ يَسْتَطِعْ فَبِقَلْبِهِ، وَذَلِكَ أَضْعَفُ الْإِيْمَانِ.

> Whoever amongst you witnesses an evil, let him reform it (practically) with his hands; if he is unable, then (let him denounce it) verbally; and if he is unable, then (let him abhor it) in his heart—and that is the weakest form of faith.[76]

This hadith mentions the levels of faith in the most beautiful manner.

Q.59. What is the beauty of *īmān*?

Ans. The actual beauty of *īmān* is that it guarantees peace and security. Becoming a believer ensures peace for the person as well as making him a source of peace for others.

Abū Hurayra ؓ narrates that the Prophet ﷺ said:

اَلْمُؤْمِنُ مَنْ أَمِنَهُ النَّاسُ عَلَى دِمَائِهِمْ وَأَمْوَالِهِمْ.

> A believer is the one that people find their blood and wealth safe from him.[77]

---

[76] Narrated by Muslim in *al-Ṣaḥīḥ: Kitāb al-īmān* (Book of Faith), 1:69 §49.

[77] Narrated by al-Nasāʾī in *al-Sunan: Kitāb al-īmān wa sharāʾiʿhī* (Book of Faith and its Codes), 8:76, §4995.

Q.60. Does *Īmān* increase or decrease?

Ans. *Īmān* is a single unit which does not accept divisions. In itself, *īmān* is not subject to increase or decrease. However, it is strengthened or weakened by our deeds. Righteous deeds and acts of piety increase its potency and influence in our lives whereas evil deeds, mischief and corruption lead it to decline and failure. The following verse asserts that the faith of a believer increases in strength with the help of good deeds.

ٱلَّذِينَ قَالَ لَهُمُ ٱلنَّاسُ إِنَّ ٱلنَّاسَ قَدْ جَمَعُواْ لَكُمْ فَٱخْشَوْهُمْ فَزَادَهُمْ إِيمَٰنًا وَقَالُواْ حَسْبُنَا ٱللَّهُ وَنِعْمَ ٱلْوَكِيلُ.

They are the ones whom people said: 'The adversaries have gathered (in great number) against you, so fear them.' But this (information) further enhanced their faith and they proclaimed: 'Allah is Sufficient for us and what an excellent Guardian He is!'[78]

Another verse relates:

إِنَّمَا ٱلْمُؤْمِنُونَ ٱلَّذِينَ إِذَا ذُكِرَ ٱللَّهُ وَجِلَتْ قُلُوبُهُمْ وَإِذَا تُلِيَتْ عَلَيْهِمْ ءَايَٰتُهُۥ زَادَتْهُمْ إِيمَٰنًا وَعَلَىٰ رَبِّهِمْ يَتَوَكَّلُونَ. ٱلَّذِينَ يُقِيمُونَ ٱلصَّلَوٰةَ وَمِمَّا رَزَقْنَٰهُمْ يُنفِقُونَ. أُوْلَٰٓئِكَ هُمُ ٱلْمُؤْمِنُونَ حَقًّا لَّهُمْ دَرَجَٰتٌ عِندَ رَبِّهِمْ وَمَغْفِرَةٌ وَرِزْقٌ كَرِيمٌ.

The believers are only those whose hearts, when Allah is mentioned (before them), are filled with awe (at the very idea of Allah's Greatness and Might). And when His Revelations are recited to them, they (i.e. the ecstatic, delightful, sweet and sublime Words of the Beloved) increase their

---

[78] Qur'ān 3:173.

faith, and they (maintain) their trust in their Lord alone (under all circumstances and do not look towards anyone other than Him). (They) are those who establish Prayer and spend (in the cause of Allah) out of whatever We have bestowed upon them. It is they who are (in fact) the true believers. For them are (high) ranks with their Lord and forgiveness and an honourable provision.[79]

Anas b. Mālik 🙭 narrates that the Prophet 🙼 said, 'Whoever confirms "there is no god but Allah" will be ultimately liberated from Hell, even if the amount of *īmān* he holds in his heart is as little as a mustard seed. Whoever confirms "there is no god but Allah" will be ultimately liberated from Hell, even if the amount of *īmān* he holds in his heart is as little as a wheat grain. Whoever confirms "there is no god but Allah" will be ultimately liberated from Hell, even if the amount of *īmān* he holds in his heart is as little as an atom. Whoever says "there is no god but Allah" will ultimately be liberated from Hell and admitted to Paradise even he could say it only once in his life.'[80]

Q.61. HOW CAN WE SAFEGUARD OUR *ĪMĀN* DURING DECADENT TIMES OF RELIGIOUS DETERIORATION— LIKE TODAY?

ANS. It is possible for the believers to save their *īmān* from destruction today if they manage to establish a strong relationship in three dimensions.

1. Relationship with Allah 🙭 (*taʿalluq bi Allāh*)

---

[79] Ibid., 8:2–4.
[80] Narrated by al-Bukhārī in *al-Ṣaḥīḥ: Kitāb al-īmān* (Book of Faith), 1:24 §44.

2. Relationship with the Messenger ﷺ (*taʿalluq bi al-rasūl*)
3. Relationship with the Qurʾān (*taʿalluq bi al-Qurʾān*)

Allah ﷻ says:

وَكَيْفَ تَكْفُرُونَ وَأَنتُمْ تُتْلَىٰ عَلَيْكُمْ ءَايَٰتُ ٱللَّهِ وَفِيكُمْ رَسُولُهُۥ وَمَن يَعْتَصِم بِٱللَّهِ فَقَدْ هُدِىَ إِلَىٰ صِرَٰطٍ مُّسْتَقِيمٍ.

> And how will you disbelieve (now) while you are (fortunate) ones to whom the Verses of Allah are recited, and the Messenger of Allah ﷺ is (himself) present among you? And whoever holds fast to (the Embrace of) Allah is most surely guided to the straight path.[81]

This verse advises every Muslim who wants to protect his/her *īmān* against disbelief and misguidance that he/she must work hard on strengthening these three attachments, for it is impossible to lose faith with all three bonds in sound condition. On the other hand, losing any one of them leads to the loss of *īmān* itself.

Q.62. What does it mean to have a sound relationship with Allah ﷻ?

Ans. It means that one does not find any place in his heart for any love other than that of Allah, ﷻ for the heart, full of love for Allah, cannot have such relationship with anybody else. Such a state of heart submits the love of wife, husband, children, sisters, brothers, relatives and friends to this great love. As a result, only the love that this great love wants to keep can stay and all the rest vanishes.

Abū Dharr al-Ghifārī ؓ narrates that the Prophet ﷺ said:

---

[81] Qurʾān 3:101.

إِنَّ أَحَبَّ الْأَعْمَالِ إِلَى اللهِ: اَلْحُبُّ فِي اللهِ وَالْبُغْضُ فِي اللهِ.

> The most beloved deed to Allah ﷻ is to love and hate for His sake.[82]

Another hadith says:

أَوْثَقُ عُرَى الْإِيْمَانِ اَلْحُبُّ فِي اللهِ وَالْبُغْضُ فِي اللهِ.

> To love and hate for the sake of Allah is the most reliable attachment of *īmān*.[83]

Q.63. What does it mean to have a sound relationship with the Messenger ﷺ?

Ans. To establish a strong attachment with the very personage of the Messenger ﷺ and to follow his teachings with one's heart and soul is called 'relationship with the Messenger ﷺ'.

Allah ﷻ says:

وَٱلَّذِينَ ءَامَنُواْ وَعَمِلُواْ ٱلصَّٰلِحَٰتِ وَءَامَنُواْ بِمَا نُزِّلَ عَلَىٰ مُحَمَّدٍ وَهُوَ ٱلْحَقُّ مِن رَّبِّهِمْ.

> And those who embrace faith and do pious works persistently and believe in this (Book) which has been revealed to Muhammad (ﷺ) and that is the very Truth from their Lord.[84]

It is sad to see that, in our present situation, we completely fail to fulfil the requirements of the high and loud proclamations of extreme love for the Prophet ﷺ

---

[82] Narrated by Aḥmad b. Ḥanbal in *al-Musnad*, 5:146; al-Ṭayālasī in *al-Musnad*, 101 §747; and Daylamī in *al-Firdaws bi-māthūr al-khiṭāb*, 1:355 §1429 and 2:155 §2786.

[83] Narrated by Ibn Abī Shayba in *al-Muṣannaf*, 6:170 §§30420–30421, 6:172 §30443; and 7:80 §34338.

[84] Qur'ān 47:2.

that we raise. The revival of the relationship with the Messenger, ﷺ ﷺ ﷺ means to adorn our necks with the most decent necklace of humble servitude to him in such a fashion that we rid ourselves of all yokes of slavery. For those who humble themselves by the servitude to our master Muhammad ﷺ are courageous enough to easily shatter the idols of fake ranks and positions as well as deceitful worldly loyalties. Such people would never acknowledge any relationship more dear than that of the noblest of all the Prophets ﷺ. Nor would they derive tranquillity from singing anybody else's praise. The day we become true and pure servants of our beloved Prophet ﷺ, we shall succeed in liberating ourselves from the awful slaveries of worldliness and arrive at the proud destination of true freedom.

Q.64. What does it mean to establish a relationship with the Qurʾān?

Ans. It means to have complete and unshakable faith that the teachings of the Qurʾān are the final truth; that we follow them in practice; that success and triumph are practically guaranteed in this world as well as in the Hereafter if we follow its teachings. Allah ﷻ says:

وَنَزَّلْنَا عَلَيْكَ ٱلْكِتَٰبَ تِبْيَٰنًا لِّكُلِّ.

> And We have revealed to you that Glorious Book which is a clear exposition of everything.[85]

This verse explains that we won't need any guidance from any philosophy or ism, except for the knowledge and wisdom that Allah ﷻ has conferred upon us in His Book the Qurʾān, if we managed to establish a true relationship with the Qurʾān. All worldly thoughts, ideologies, philosophies and systems are useless, deficient

---

[85] Ibid., 16:89.

and obliterated. What we actually need is simply to comport ourselves according to the Qur'ānic matrix in such a manner that we abstain from what Qur'ān forbids and perform what it enjoins. Only then will our relationship with the Qur'ān be established.

The Qur'ān has declared that the protection of *īmān* depends upon establishing these three devotions which constitute the foundation of faith. Unless we belong to Allah, His Prophet Muhammad ﷺ and the Qur'ān in a true relationship of guidance, servitude and worship established in the best of manners, we can't be assured of the protection of our *īmān*.

Q.65. What is the criterion to judge the rectitude of *īmān*?

Ans. Allah ﷻ leads His servants through different conditions and situations in order to judge their state of *īmān*. The following verse states clearly that Allah ﷻ puts them through five types of tribulations to try their firmness upon faith.

وَلَنَبْلُوَنَّكُم بِشَيْءٍ مِّنَ ٱلْخَوْفِ وَٱلْجُوعِ وَنَقْصٍ مِّنَ ٱلْأَمْوَالِ وَٱلْأَنفُسِ
وَٱلثَّمَرَاتِ وَبَشِّرِ ٱلصَّٰبِرِينَ.

> And We will most certainly test you somewhat by means of fear and hunger and certain loss of wealth and lives and fruits. And, (O Beloved,) give glad tidings to those who observe patience.[86]

This verse mentions five kinds of tribulations. The standard behaviour of firm faith in the case of any of them would be to bear with patience and go back to Allah ﷻ wholeheartedly instead of going astray.

---

[86] Ibid., 2:155.

Q.66. What is the first kind of tribulation of rectitude?

Ans. The first tribulation is 'fear'. It covers human life like a pall. A man goes through tests and tribulation all his life, surrounded by dangers, anxieties, concerns, fears that keep hovering around. At times one fears for one's life, for the loss of property or money, or is anxious about children getting out of hand, concerned about the future, one's chastity, defamation by others. The main point here is to observe the state of our relationship with Allah ﷻ and how firmly it adheres to the Lord during hard times of tribulation! If it remains firm throughout all circumstances of fear, we must thank Allah ﷻ that He did help us to pass the trial.

Q.67. What is the second tribulation of rectitude?

Ans. The second one is hunger. Believers will have to live a hard life of hunger. It is not because Allah ﷻ is not aware of their needs or holds some hostility against them. It is rather to try how they keep their faith unshaken when the times are harsh for their stomachs.

Q.68. What is the third tribulation of rectitude?

Ans. The third one is 'reduction of wealth'. This means that sometimes a servant is deprived of all the blessings, wealth and material ease he has been provided. The purpose being to judge the state of his faith in both affluence and scarcity, to see whether he breaks his relationship with Allah ﷻ after losing worldly affluence and turns to others than Allah in denial of His divinity.

Q.69. What is the fourth tribulation of rectitude?

Ans. It is 'reduction of souls'. It appears in the form of loss of life. It also includes trying a person through the afflictions of harm and disease—of different levels of severity. Even the agonies of death are a kind of trial. One is tested whether one longs to attend the divine countenance or prefers to remain in this world.

Q.70. What is the fifth tribulation of rectitude?

Ans. It is 'reduction of fruits', which refers particularly to the death of one's children. Some people are kept deprived of children, which is a test of their forbearance. Others are given children, which is a test whether the excess of affection for children makes them unmindful of Allah ﷻ. So are the cases of giving children and then taking them back, giving daughters without sons or giving sons without daughters. Such are all different forms of tribulations that we observe in our daily life. They are like a furnace to brighten faith as pure gold.

Q.71. What does 'the branches of *īmān*' mean?

Ans. This term refers to different deeds. A person, no matter what sphere of life he belongs to, can obtain divine proximity if he performs his duties sincerely and abiding by the principles of Shariah. The following verse explains the same point:

وَٱلَّذِينَ جَٰهَدُواْ فِينَا لَنَهْدِيَنَّهُمْ سُبُلَنَا.

> And those who toil hard (and fight the lower self vehemently) for Our cause We certainly guide

> them in Our Ways (of striving for and attaining to the gnosis—*al-sayr* and *al-wuṣūl*).[87]

Let's not ignore the fact that the verse does not say that those who strive hard are guided to 'one way'. It rather mentions many passages. It means that there are great many paths available to mankind in life. So, each individual can choose the path that suits his heartfelt and spiritual state.

Abū Hurayra ﵁ narrates that the Prophet ﷺ said:

> '*Īmān* has more than 70 branches. The most superior of them is to utter *lā ilāha ill Allāh* and the lowest one is to remove inconvenience from a passage. Prudency and modesty is also an incredible branch of *īmān*.'[88]

This hadith asserts positively that each branch holds a very important place and definitely earns the person who observes it, Allah's proximity because it is a blessing.

Q.72. How many manners does *īmān* have and what are they?

Ans. The fundamental manners of *īmān* are 3 and it is essential to perform them in order to be a believer:

1. The first manner of *īmān* for a Muslim is to consider the whole of life as a single unit and a totality whose portions are inseparably joined together. It requires that one does not allow anything to involve one of its portions with faith and the other with disbelief, for then it would be a mixture of belief and disbelief, which has been declared hypocrisy by the Qur'ān.

---

[87] Ibid., 29:69.

[88] Narrated by Muslim in *al-Ṣaḥīḥ: Kitāb al-īmān* [Book of Faith], 1:63 §58.

2. The second manner of *īmān* is never to draw even close to the limits prescribed by the Qur'ān and hadith. This requires a clear distinction between *ḥalāl* and *ḥarām* to work in our life in a fashion that leaves no shadow of disbelief and hypocrisy. Moreover, both the secular and religious matters of our life are settled within the frame of Islamic teachings in a manner that leaves behind no conflict between the inner and the outer human personality. It also renders human personality and life free of doubt.

3. The third manner of *īmān* is to embrace Islam as a policy/practice for life, as the Qur'ān has commanded to enforce it in our life. This requires sincere faith in submitting to each directive and practice from the *sīra* of the Prophet ﷺ openheartedly and without the slightest of doubts. It also requires us to reject whatever we find against the Qur'ān and Sunna like we reject disbelief. This actually is the basic condition of *īmān*.

Q.73. Why have contemporary Muslims in general, and the youth in particular, lost the efficacy of *īmān*?

ANS. The basic reasons include a lack of awareness of the meaning of *īmān* among the younger generation and an overall failure of meeting its requirements as well as fulfilling its conditions. Moreover, a three-pronged assault of anti-Islam forces on ideological, cultural and emotional fronts has also caused younger Muslims—in particular—to lose the influence of *īmān* in their lives as it has done with the *Umma* in general. For it is a fact beyond dispute that ideology forms the foundation of the building of a nation, religion, movement or organisation. It is also an equally important fact that nations continue to survive on the basis of their ideology. As soon as the ideological foundation of a nation begins to lose its strength, it falls victim to decline, incertitude and doubt.

A simple analogy to grasp the point would be that of a tree. A tree's life, growth, blossoming and flourishing depend upon its roots. If its roots happen to sustain some damage, the tree will begin to wither. Its leaves, branches, flowers and fruit will gradually grow rotten. Strong roots, on the other hand, not only make the tree strong and fruitful, they also make it a source of food and life for others. It all depends upon the efficacy. The roots and trunk run their influence through the whole tree; producing bright fruits and beautiful flowers when healthy and causing wither and decay when unhealthy. Likewise, in the case of ideology, it serves as the source of cultural, religious and social survival of nations.

This is why the Muslim *Umma* will have to adopt its own basic ideology and comport its life within the frame of Islamic teachings, if it wants to taste the sweetness of *īmān* and develop itself as a nation. Otherwise, it will be destined to humiliation, lowliness, inferiority and oppression. The Qur'ān says:

إِنَّ ٱللَّهَ لَا يُغَيِّرُ مَا بِقَوْمٍ حَتَّىٰ يُغَيِّرُوا۟ مَا بِأَنفُسِهِمْ.

> Verily, Allah does not change the state of a people until they bring about a change in themselves.[89]

Q.74. What is the ideological assault and how can we guard against it?

Ans. The ideological attack is increasing the distance between the younger Muslim generation and Islam on an intellectual front. It draws support from deviant notions

[89] Qur'ān 13:11.

and false concepts. Unarmed with proper religious education, these young ones, when they reach college and university where they study western philosophies and ideologies, neglect their religious teachings and find themselves lost into the labyrinthine corridors of complex materialistic opinions and isms. As a result, their faith in the unseen, the Hereafter, prophecy, and messengership grows weak. Immature young minds, then, not only turn a deaf ear to the teachings of the Qur'ān and the hadith, they also begin to lose their confidence in the practicability of Islamic concepts. All this because of the ideological assault that anti-Islam forces continue to launch against the hearts and souls of Muslims.

The best option in the course of guarding against this attack is to present Islam through solid scientific reasoning in order to restore their confidence that there is no system other than Islam that can withstand philosophical, inferential and practical argumentation based on the most modern scientific developments. They need to be reminded that the modern philosophies and isms are based on materialism, whereas Islamic philosophy springs from the fountain of the divine teachings of the Qur'ān and the Holy personage of our beloved Prophet Muhammad ﷺ. We cannot bring our youth back to Islam or strengthen their *īmān* by issuing religious edicts or instilling the fear of Hell. We rather need to persuade them by presenting *īmān* and Islam to them in a fashion that rebuilds their confidence in the Qur'ān and the hadith to be the real source of solutions to today's problems. If such a strategy is adopted, we shall see the foundation of the younger generation's *īmān* growing stronger and stronger instead of being shaken. Iqbāl says:

Nahīn hay nā ummīd Iqbāl apnī kasht-e-wīrān say

> *Zarā nam ho to ye matti baRī zarkhayz hay sāqī*
>
> 'Iqbāl is not disappointed by his desolate farm (the hearts and souls of Muslim *Umma*).
>
> 'If just a little moist, this soil (the hearts of Muslim *Umma* to produce the fruits of faith) is very fertile, O Cupbearer (Allah and His Messenger ﷺ)!'

A realistic contemporary study of Islam and practising its teachings is the only way to tackle the negative effects of this assault, which lands on the *īmān* of the *Umma* by aiming at its intellect.

Q.75. What does cultural attack mean and how can we guard against it?

Ans. It stands for the assault that appears in the form of (the wide spread of) Western culture, whose influence is causing a radical change in the younger generation's thoughts about social and economic life. Moral, family and social values are growing weaker, so much so that a huge wave of impudence, immodesty, indecency, obscenity and dissoluteness has overwhelmed the whole of society. The matter has fallen victim to decadence to the extent that girls have forgotten to feel embarrassed at all while strolling around the house without being bashful in front of elders, let alone covering their heads. This Western cultural assault has moulded all social values in a dangerous direction and given it the name of so-called fashion and modernity. As a result of a loosened hold of Shariah, Islam (being Muslim) departed from our lives to leave us Muslims in name only. Our Islamic identity laments our loss of Islam with a deep sigh. Iqbāl expresses it in a couplet that means:

> *Waḍaᶜ main tum ho Nasārā, to tamaddun main hanūd.*

Tum Musalman ho, jinhayn dekh kay sharmayen yahūd

> 'You have adopted the look of Christians and culture of Hindus,
>
> 'Do you really think you are Muslims? Even Jews are embarrassed by your degree of corruption in religion!"

The very first step to ensure protection against this attack is to establish a strong and deep relationship of extreme love and heartfelt bonding, among Muslims in general and their youth in particular, with the *sīra* and Sunna of our Prophet ﷺ as well as to portray Islam for them in an attractive way. At the same time, it should also be explained to them that the great examples of high and purposeful life, as well as of culture and the system of moral values, with which the Messenger to mankind and the guide of absolute truth has provided us, are practically the best and the most virtuous in the whole world. It is the most important task of our times to bring proper and appropriate information of the principles and cultural values of Islam to the younger generation. By raising their children and casting their minds and behaviour according to non-Islamic cultural frames from their childhood, some parents are also playing a negative role in the weakening of Islamic values as much as the anti-Islam forces. Matters are subject to their times of execution. You can mould it the way you want when the iron is red hot. Once it is cold and solid for your remissness, it can no longer be subject to any changes. The duty of protecting the precious assets of unique values, manifest in Islamic culture, also rests upon the shoulders of our religious scholars, Imams of mosques, literary people, poets and writers as a prime responsibility. It is incumbent upon them to strengthen the traditions and values of Islam, in their talks, admonitions, writings and poetry, in the light of the Qur'ān and the Sunna. The Holy Prophet ﷺ said:

كُلُّكُمْ رَاعٍ وَّكُلُّكُمْ مَسْؤُوْلٌ عَنْ رَعِيَّتِهِ.

> Everybody among you is a shepherd and is responsible for his sheep.[90]

Everybody is responsible for matters within his range of influence (such as a family head for his family). If somebody's authority covers a locality, a town, a city, a province or a country, his scope of accountability covers that level of concern. What is really needed is to enforce Islam at each level, from home to locality to town to country so as to prevent the flickering lamp of the younger generation's *īmān* from going out in the tempest of modern culture.

Q.76. How can we safeguard against the attack on emotional front?

Ans. The most threatening and malignant assault in our times is being imposed upon us through voluptuous pleasures. Unfortunately, our youngsters are rather miserable victims of carnal sensuality. Assemblies of wine-consumption and dancing at places and night clubs are commonplace in Muslim countries. Impudent movies everywhere from hotels to cinemas to mini cinemas to houses, with audacious brazenness, have landed heavy blows upon the morality of the masses. Media, in the form of immoral broadcasts through cable, internet and other means, continue to set adrift the purity, pudencies, and modesty of our sons and daughters at home, like a flood sweeping away powerless sticks and straws.

---

[90] Narrated by al-Bukhārī in *al-Ṣaḥīḥ: Kitāb al-nikāḥ* (Book of Marriage), 5:1988 §4892.

In short, the emotional attack has shattered the very foundations of *īmān*. The younger generation, males and females, are consequently falling prey to immorality. This is why the Muslim Umma, having fallen far from Islamic teachings, manifests decline and is bound to lead a life of ideological and political misery.

Once the decadence takes place on the emotional front, it cannot be cured by listening to lectures and reading books for they only knock at the doors of conscience. Admonitions cannot force their way into the heart when the mind is troubled with perplexity. When your heart is restless and your soul is full of anxiety, you cannot be enchanted by Ṣalāh, Ṣawm or remembrance of Allah ﷻ. The only workable method of guarding against the emotional assault in this situation would be the restoration of a sentimental and spiritual relationship with Allah ﷻ and the Prophet Muhammad ﷺ, which is only possible through adopting *taṣawwuf*, Islamic spiritualism and the company of the righteous, for the training method with them is quite different. They don't burden those who draw closer to them with a long list of do's and don'ts or knock them under a pile of books in the early stages. They just set alight a spark of love for their Lord which makes them restless and their hearts incline to Allah and they begin to see the light of *īmān*. Once the value of *īmān* begins to settle in the heart and the feelings gradually incline towards guidance, they are made aware of the rulings of Shariah and given responsibility for deeds. The prospect of regaining the lost wealth of the *Dīn* and *īmān* can easily be brightened for today's Umma, as they are in decline, and the deterioration can be remedied, if this spirit is revitalised.

Q.77. What is the value of the relationship with the Prophet ﷺ in *Īmān*?

Ans. *Īmān*, actually, is the name of establishing a heartfelt relationship with the Holy Prophet ﷺ. If this is not acquired, the access to the status of *īmān* cannot be assumed.

The Holy Prophet ﷺ has clearly stated:

> 'None of you can ever be a perfect believer unless he loves me more dearly than his father, his children and all other people.'[91]

This hadith explicitly confirms that the only criterion to judge *īmān* is to hold the person of Muhammad ﷺ more dear than the whole universe. Unless this quality is instilled, a person can be a Muslim but not a *muʾmin* (perfect believer).

Once ʿUmar b. al-Khaṭṭāb ؓ was in the presence of the Prophet ﷺ when the Prophet ﷺ asked him how much he # loved him ﷺ. ʿUmar ؓ, who was still going through some of the phases of training, replied that he loved the Prophet ﷺ more than anybody else, except that he felt that he loved himself more. The Prophet ﷺ said his *īmān* was not yet complete in that case. These words of the Prophet ﷺ changed the condition of ʿUmar's ؓ heart and the love of the Prophet ﷺ dominated all other loves. He ؓ spontaneously said, 'By Allah! Now I love you more

---

[91] Narrated by al-Bukhārī in *al-Ṣaḥīḥ: Kitab al-īmān* [Book of Faith], chapter: 'Love of the Messenger ﷺ is from faith', 1:14 §14.

than myself.' At this, the Prophet ﷺ held his hand and said, 'Now, your *īmān* if perfected O ʿUmar!'[92]

Let's not forget, here, that outer aspect of the companions of the Prophet ﷺ was not in conflict with the inner. Their character was beyond the doubts of hypocrisy. This is why ʿUmar ؓ expressed what he felt in his heart, when the Prophet ﷺ asked him.

Q.78. WHICH DEEDS OF THE PROPHET'S COMPANIONS HELPED THEM ACHIEVE THE HIGHEST RANK OF *ĪMĀN*?

ANS. It was not due to their deeds. They actually had comported themselves within the frame of the Sunna to the best of their ability. This was something that made them models of perfection for the believers till the Last Day. The companionship of the Prophet ﷺ was their very privilege and an honour to distinguish them above all humans on Earth. It was evidence that they sacrificed every relationship they had for their relationship with the Prophet ﷺ as well as all dimensions and nobilities of their personalities for the companionship of their beloved ﷺ.

This is exactly what the Qurʾān has emphasised about those devoted and dedicated people:

مُّحَمَّدٌ رَّسُولُ ٱللَّهِ وَٱلَّذِينَ مَعَهُ أَشِدَّآءُ عَلَى ٱلْكُفَّارِ رُحَمَآءُ بَيْنَهُمْ تَرَىٰهُمْ رُكَّعًا سُجَّدًا يَبْتَغُونَ فَضْلاً مِّنَ ٱللَّهِ وَرِضْوَانًا.

Muhammad (ﷺ) is the Messenger of Allah. And those with him are hard and tough against the disbelievers but kind-hearted and merciful among themselves. You see them excessively

---

[92] Narrated by al-Bukhārī in *al-Ṣaḥīḥ: Kitāb al-īmān* [Book of Faith], 6:2445 §6257.

> bowing and prostrating themselves. They simply seek Allah's grace and pleasure.[93]

This verse highlights the aspect of their conduct which became a brilliant example for their obedience and devotion to the noblest Prophet ﷺ.

Q.79. Which comes first from *īmān* and actions?

Ans. *Īmān* comes before action. It is just like the root is prior to the plant. No action is acceptable without *īmān*. Righteous deeds are spiritual diet for the strength of *īmān* and do not qualify as liberators from disbelief. If they do not accompany *īmān* they are useless for their performer would still be in the state of disbelief. The Qur'ān confirms:

أُوْلَٰٓئِكَ ٱلَّذِينَ كَفَرُواْ بِـَٔايَٰتِ رَبِّهِمْ وَلِقَآئِهِۦ فَحَبِطَتْ أَعْمَٰلُهُمْ فَلَا نُقِيمُ لَهُمْ يَوْمَ ٱلْقِيَٰمَةِ وَزْنًا.

> It is they who have denied the Signs of their Lord and meeting Him (after death). So all their deeds are ruined, and We shall not give any weight or (even) any worth to them on the Day of Rising.[94]

This divine declaration confirms the superiority of *īmān* above action. Being faithless will account for eternal loss for a person in the life hereafter.

Q.80. What is the status of bodily actions in *īmān*?

Ans. *Īmān*, indeed, is the name for testimony in the heart. Bodily deeds are originally not part of *īmān*,

---

[93] Qur'ān 48:29.

[94] Ibid., 18:105.

although they are certainly required for its perfection. If a person is responsible for the deeds, which breach the faith completely, such as worshipping idols, the Moon, the Sun or anything else, or showing disrespect for a prophet, the Qur'ān, the sanctioned Kaʿba or some practice of the Prophet ﷺ, he would definitely be declared a non-believer. Anyone who happens to carry out such a deed is required to accept Islam anew, and remarry his wife if he was married prior to its commission.

Q.81. What is the definition of a believer?

Ans. A believer is a person who has the quality of faith. His/her heart submits to Allah ﷻ without the least of doubts about Allah and His Messenger ﷺ.

Q.82. How many kinds of believers are there?

Ans. There are two kinds of believers.

1. Practising (righteous – good doer)
2. Non-practising (transgressors/disobedient ones)

A righteous believer is the believer who, along with verbal assertion and heartfelt verification of faith, abides by the rulings of Shariah and obeys the commands of Allah ﷻ and His Messenger ﷺ. He does not behave against the commissions and omissions of Shariah.

A disobedient believer, on the other hand, is a believer whose conduct is against the rulings of Shariah despite his verbal assertion and heartfelt verification of faith. For example those Muslims who believe that Ṣalāh and Ṣawm are obligations of Shariah but do not perform them. Such people are disobedient believers.

Q.83. What qualities are attributed to believers in the hadith?

Ans.

1. The true believer (*mu'min*) is he whom people trust with regard to their blood and their properties.[95]
2. A believer is another believer's brother. He is not allowed to spoil another believer's financial dealings. [For example, to make an offer to the seller after the first one has bought something and the deal has been finalised.][96]
3. The most perfect *īmān* is that of the one whose moral conduct is the most refined.[97]

4. Allah ﷻ has enjoined 7 rights upon a believer towards other believers.

1) To love him
2) To respect him
3) To spend on him from his wealth
4) Not to backbite against him
5) To visit him when he is ill
6) To attend his funeral
7) To talk well of him after his death.[98]

5. A true believer will spend his wealth upon the needy and be just to them.[99]

---

[95] Narrated by al-Nasā'ī in *al-Sunan: Kitāb al-Īmān wa sharā'iʿuhu* [The Book of Faith and its Revealed Laws], chapter: 'The Quality of the True Believer', 8:104 §4995; and Aḥmad b. Ḥanbal in al-Musnad, 2:379 §8918.

[96] Narrated by Muslim in *al-Ṣaḥīḥ: Kitāb al-nikāḥ* [Book of Marriage], 2:1034 §1414.

[97] Narrated by al-Tirmidhī in *al-Sunan*: *Kitāb al-raḍāʿa* [The Book of Suckling], chapter: 'What Has Come to Us About the Wife's Right upon Her Husband', 3:466 §1162; Aḥmad b. Ḥanbal in *al-Musnad*, 2:472 §10110; Ibn Ḥibbān in *al-Ṣaḥīḥ*, 2:227 §479; al-Ḥākim in *al-Mustadrak*, 1:43 §2; al-Dārimī in *al-Sunan*, 2:415 §2792; and Abū Yaʿlā in *al-Musnad*, 7:237 §4240.

[98] Narrated by Ibn Bābawayh in *Kitāb al-khisāl*, pp. 364–365.

6. A believer is the mirror of the other believer. He corrects him if sees any fault in him.[100]

7. The Prophet ﷺ said, 'Killing a believer is a more serious matter in the sight of God than the destruction of the entire world.'[101]

Some of the other qualities that have been attributed to believers in a number of prophetic traditions include that they are brothers of one another; they should live in mutual harmony; share grief and happiness; and avoid backbiting and other social evils.

Q.84. What grades of *Īmān* does Allah ﷻ give to believers?

Ans. If a believer keeps faithful to Allah ﷻ and His Messenger ﷺ truly and fulfils all the requirements firmly, Allah ﷻ not only bestows upon him the grade of *ṣiddīqiyya* (truthfulness) but also confers upon him the rank of a martyr without having sacrificed his life because he is considered as bearing the truest and the most sincere witness of Allah's oneness. The Qur'ān states:

وَٱلَّذِينَ ءَامَنُوا۟ بِٱللَّهِ وَرُسُلِهِۦٓ أُو۟لَٰٓئِكَ هُمُ ٱلصِّدِّيقُونَ وَٱلشُّهَدَآءُ عِندَ رَبِّهِمْ لَهُمْ أَجْرُهُمْ وَنُورُهُمْ.

[99] ʿIzz al-Dīn al-Balīq said in *Minhāj al-ṣāliḥīn* (p. 91) that al-Ṭaḥāwī had narrated it.

[100] Narrated by Abū Dāwūd in *al-Sunan: Kitāb al-diyāt* [Book of Blood-money], 4:285 §4918; and al-Bayhaqī in *al-Sunan al-kubrā*, 8:167 §16458.

[101] Narrated by al-Nasāʾī in *al-Sunan*: *Kitāb taḥrīm al-dam* [The Book on the Prohibition of Bloodshed], chapter: 'The Sanctity of Blood', 7:82–83 §§3988–3990; al-Ṭabarānī in *al-Muʿjam al-ṣaghīr*, 1:355 §594; and al-Bayhaqī in *al-Sunan al-kubrā*, 8:22 §15647. Imam al-Ṭabarānī declared this tradition authentic [*ḥasan*].

> And those who believe in Allah and His Messengers are *al-ṣiddiqūn* (the Champions of Truth) and *al-shuhadāʾ* (the Faithful Witnesses) in the sight of their Lord. For them is their reward and their light (as well).[102]

Allah ﷻ grants two shares of His mercy to those who fear God and have faith in His Beloved ﷺ and gratifies them with light through His blessings, and His guidance replaces misguidance for them. Even on the Day of Judgement, this light will be around them to show them the way. The Qurʾān states:

يَٰٓأَيُّهَا ٱلَّذِينَ ءَامَنُوا۟ ٱتَّقُوا۟ ٱللَّهَ وَءَامِنُوا۟ بِرَسُولِهِۦ يُؤْتِكُمْ كِفْلَيْنِ مِن رَّحْمَتِهِۦ وَيَجْعَل لَّكُمْ نُورًا تَمْشُونَ بِهِۦ وَيَغْفِرْ لَكُمْ وَٱللَّهُ غَفُورٌ رَّحِيمٌ.

> O Believers! Become God-fearing and believe in His (Esteemed) Messenger (ﷺ). He will bless you with two portions of His Mercy and will bring about light for you to walk in (in the world and in the Hereafter) and will forgive you. And Allah is Most Forgiving, Ever-Merciful.[103]

Q.85. If somebody utters a word of disbelief under extreme coercion, will he lose his faith?

Ans. No. If somebody is coerced to the extreme that he fears for his life, then he will not lose his faith. He has a concession to save his life provided that disbelief does not go beyond utterance and he is satisfied with faith. The Qurʾān has an explicit declaration:

---

[102] Qurʾān 57:19.
[103] Ibid., 57:28.

مَن كَفَرَ بِٱللَّهِ مِنۢ بَعْدِ إِيمَٰنِهِۦٓ إِلَّا مَنْ أُكْرِهَ وَقَلْبُهُۥ مُطْمَئِنٌّۢ بِٱلْإِيمَٰنِ وَلَٰكِن مَّن شَرَحَ بِٱلْكُفْرِ صَدْرًا فَعَلَيْهِمْ غَضَبٌ مِّنَ ٱللَّهِ وَلَهُمْ عَذَابٌ عَظِيمٌ.

The one who disbelieves after having believed, except someone who is coercively forced to do so and at heart remains contented with belief (as before), but (of course) he who (adopts) disbelief (afresh) wholeheartedly with an open mind, on them is wrath from Allah and for them is fierce torment.[104]

Q.86. Who is called hypocrite?

Ans. A *munāfiq* (hypocrite) is a person who asserts his faith in Allah ﷻ and His Messenger ﷺ but does not accept it in his heart.

Q.87. What are the signs of a hypocrite?

Ans. Hypocrisy is a behaviour that founds itself upon conflict between word and action. The outward appearance of a hypocrite is different from his inner self to the extent of total disagreement. Verses 8 to 20 of *sūra al-baqara* represent an emblematic description of hypocrisy. The latter is rather a clear charter of hypocrisy. It provides us with a chance to reflect upon ourselves in its light and mend our ways for a pure and strong faith. We mention them here.

1. To proclaim faith verbally with the heart empty of it.
2. To consider the faith in God's unity and Hereafter sufficient and believe that the faith in Prophet Muhammad's ﷺ messengership is not indispensible.
3. To have a psyche of deception and fraudulence.

---

[104] Ibid., 16:106.

4. To think that Allah ﷻ and His Messenger Muhammad ﷺ are unaware of their state of hypocrisy.
5. To believe in the success of their fraudulence and deception in fooling others.
6. To be sick at heart—unable to accept the truth.
7. To tell lies.
8. To consider themselves to be reformists despite their corrupt conduct behind the veil of correction.
9. To assume others to be foolish and consider oneself as intellectual.
10. To believe the majority of Muslims to be misguided.
11. Not to follow the consensus of the Umma—or its vast majority.
12. To be two-faced and hold conflicting inner and outer aspects.
13. To prepare conspiracies and destructive plans against the people of truth
14. To ridicule Muslims and despise them and show reproachful and taunting behaviour towards them.
15. To prefer falsehood to truth.
16. To turn a blind eye to the truth despite its clarity.
17. The inability of the tongue to speak the truth, the ears to hear the truth and the eyes to see the truth because of narrow-mindedness and hostility.
18. To be dismayed and unnerved when faced with hard times in the course of working for Islam and finding excuses to avoid them.
19. To be perplexed at the success of the people of the truth and envy them.
20. To befriend the people of truth and support them for worldly gain and depart them to avoid sacrifice when in dangers and tribulations.
21. To remain in a state of apathy and dejection about the truth.

Q.88. What is the difference between *mu'min*, Muslim and *munāfiq*?

Ans.

1. The foundation of being a *mu'min* is to declare the word of the truth with the tongue and confirm it in the heart. He/she is a person whose heart has fully submitted to Allah ﷿.
2. Being a Muslim depends upon deeds and obedience. He/she is a person whose appearance submits to Allah ﷿.
3. *Munāfiq* has an appearance which is the opposite of his/her inner nature. He/she is a person whose heart has not even accepted what he/she asserts.

Q.89. Who is a *murtadd* (an apostate)?

Ans. A Muslim who accepts disbelief and remains confirmed in it is called a *murtadd*.

Q.90. Who is called a *kāfir* (disbeliever)?

Ans. A *kāfir* is a person who neither accepts *īmān* in divine Unity and the Messengership of Prophet Muhammad ﷺ at heart nor asserts it.

Q.91. If people without faith perform good deeds, will they be rewarded in this world and the Hereafter?

Ans. Allah ﷿ states in the Qur'ān.

مَّثَلُ ٱلَّذِينَ كَفَرُواْ بِرَبِّهِمْ أَعْمَٰلُهُمْ كَرَمَادٍ ٱشْتَدَّتْ بِهِ ٱلرِّيحُ فِى يَوْمٍ
عَاصِفٍ لَّا يَقْدِرُونَ مِمَّا كَسَبُواْ عَلَىٰ شَىْءٍ ذَٰلِكَ هُوَ ٱلضَّلَٰلُ ٱلْبَعِيدُ.

The example of those who have rejected faith in their Lord is that their works are like ashes on which blows the strong wind on a stormy day—they are unable to grasp anything of the (works)

> that they earned. This is straying far into error.[105]

This verse exemplifies that the good deeds of the disbelievers are as a heap of ashes, blown away by a stormy wind. Good deeds without *īmān* carry no value in Allah's court.

Q.92. Whose *īmān* did the Prophet ﷺ regard as the most wonderful?

ANS. It may not be amazing if those who were the most fortunate to satisfy their eyes with the glorious countenance of the Prophet Muhammad ﷺ unveiled day in, day out, were content with the grandeur of such embodiment of subtle beauty of features and conduct—a whole body of compassion, mercy and kindness. [Although it is a great blessing because some people are too narrow-minded, prejudiced and envious to admit even after having seen the ocean flow and the sunshine.] In contrast to them, if we find those who have never seen the beloved, and yet they believe in him ﷺ, and his distinct splendour; hold his word dearly (to practice); and make him the centre of their love, hope, shelter and refuge, their state of *īmān* will not only be amazing but also marvellous and enviable. Such is the *īmān* that has been portrayed by a hadith as the Prophet ﷺ asked his Companions ﷺ:

أَيُّ الْخَلْقِ أَعْجَبُ إِلَيْكُمْ إِيْمَاناً؟

> Whose *īmān* is the most incredible in your opinion?

They replied, 'That of angels.' The Prophet ﷺ said:

---

[105] Ibid., 14:18.

وَمَا لَهُمْ لَا يُؤْمِنُوْنَ وَهُمْ عِنْدَ رَبِّهِمْ؟

Why wouldn't they believe! They live in the presence of Allah ﷻ (and are constantly busy in glorifying Him).

The Companions ﷺ said, 'Then, it is that of the Prophets ﷺ.' The Prophet ﷺ said:

وَمَالَهُمْ لَا يُؤْمِنُوْنَ وَالْوَحْيُ يَنْزِلُ عَلَيْهِمْ؟

Why wouldn't they believe! The revelation descends upon them.

The Companions ﷺ said, '(In that case) our *īmān* is the most extraordinary.' The Prophet ﷺ said:

وَمَالَكُمْ لَا تُؤْمِنُوْنَ وَأَنَا بَيْنَ أَظْهُرِكُمْ؟

Why wouldn't you believe while I am among you!

Then the Prophet ﷺ said:

أَلَا إِنَّ أَعْجَبَ الْخَلْقِ إِلَيَّ إِيْمَاناً لَقَوْمٌ يَكُوْنُوْنَ مِنْ بَعْدِي يَجِدُوْنَ صُحُفاً فِيْهَا كِتَابٌ يُؤْمِنُوْنَ بِمَا فِيْهَا.

Behold! The most incredible (and enviable) *īmān* to me is that of the people who will be after me. They will only see the pages which contain the book (of Allah) and will believe in it.[106]

Those who believe in him ﷺ and love him without even seeing him ﷺ, the beloved ﷺ is not only mindful of them but also watchful of them. He ﷺ does not privilege them now but long before they are even born. That is why

---

[106] Narrated by al-Ṭabarānī in *al-Muʿjam al-kabīr*, 12:87 §12560; and al-Ḥākim in *al-Mustadrak*, 4:96 §6993.

the Master ﷺ declared 1400 years ago that the faith of those who would come after him ﷺ among his Umma will be the most incredible.

Q.93. What does knowledge of the unseen (*ʿIlm al-ghayb*) mean?

Ans. The knowledge of the unseen means the knowledge that cannot be perceived through any means. It can only be received through Allah's blessing. It is a divine peculiarity and none other than Him ﷻ can be 'knower of the unseen'.

Q.94. Can knowledge of the unseen still be called unseen after being a divine bestowal?

Ans. Yes. It is called unseen before and after it has been given by Allah ﷻ. The Qur'ān mentions, after revealing the story of Prophet Yūsuf ﷺ to our Prophet Muhammad ﷺ:

ذَالِكَ مِنْ أَنْبَآءِ ٱلْغَيْبِ نُوحِيهِ إِلَيْكَ.

> O My Esteemed Beloved! This (narrative) is of the news of the unseen which We are revealing to you.[107]

This verse proves that the Qur'ān terms it as 'unseen' after it has been revealed to the Prophet ﷺ.

Q.95. What does *Īmān bi al-ghayb* (faith in the unseen) mean?

Ans. It means belief in the facts that Allah's Messenger ﷺ has told us without having seen (or being required to see) them.

---

[107] Qur'ān 12:102.

Q.96. In what way does Satan attack those with weak faith?

Ans. Those who are *kāfir* are already in the way of Satan. It is hard for Satan to make a successful assault on those with strong faith. The Qur᾽ān states:

قَالَ رَبِّ بِمَآ أَغْوَيْتَنِي لَأُزَيِّنَنَّ لَهُمْ فِي ٱلْأَرْضِ وَلَأُغْوِيَنَّهُمْ أَجْمَعِينَ. إِلَّا عِبَادَكَ مِنْهُمُ ٱلْمُخْلَصِينَ.

> Iblīs said: 'O Lord, because You have led me astray, I will (also) best adorn and embellish for them (the sins, revolts and violations) in the earth and will certainly lead all of them astray by all means, Except for those exalted servants of Yours who have attained freedom (from my deceits and intrigues of the ill-commanding selves).'[108]

This is why Satan succeeds in leading those with weak faith astray more quickly and frequently than those with strong faith. He has made a solemn commitment.

قَالَ فَبِمَآ أَغْوَيْتَنِي لَأَقْعُدَنَّ لَهُمْ صِرَاطَكَ ٱلْمُسْتَقِيمَ. ثُمَّ لَأٓتِيَنَّهُم مِّنْ بَيْنِ أَيْدِيهِمْ وَمِنْ خَلْفِهِمْ وَعَنْ أَيْمَٰنِهِمْ وَعَن شَمَآئِلِهِمْ وَلَا تَجِدُ أَكْثَرَهُمْ شَٰكِرِينَ.

> He (Iblīs) said: 'Since You have led me astray, (I swear that) I will (also) sit on Your straight path (to waylay the children of Ādam till I cause them to deviate from the path of Truth). I will assuredly approach them from their front, from their rear, from their right and from their left

[108] Ibid., 15:40–41.

and (consequently) You will not find most of them grateful.'[109]

Abatement of righteous deeds and their deficiency cause weakness of *īmān*. The Devil whispers doubts and insinuations into hearts with weak faith such as 'What is the reality of Divine Essence? Do Paradise and Hell really exist?' etc. Such doubts keep weakening faith and reducing certainty. Allah ﷻ says:

$$ إِنَّهُ يَرَاكُمْ هُوَ وَقَبِيلُهُ مِنْ حَيْثُ لَا تَرَوْنَهُمْ. $$

Indeed he (himself) and his clan keep watching you (from such positions where) you cannot catch sight of them.[110]

Q.97. WHO RELISHES THE SWEETNESS OF ĪMⱯN?

ANS. Anas b. Mālik ؓ narrates that the Prophet ﷺ said that there are three qualities and whoever combines them in himself shall enjoy the taste of *īmān*.

1. He loves Allah and His Messenger ﷺ more than anything else.

2. He does not love anything except for the sake of Allah ﷻ—he does not require any worldly need through it.

3. Once Allah ﷻ has liberated him from disbelief, he dreads returning to disbelief like he dreads being thrown into fire.[111]

Q.98. WHAT IS THE STANDARD OF CORRECT ĪMĀN?

ANS. The criterion of true *īmān* is that the servants of Allah ﷻ connect themselves to the worship of Allah ﷻ

---

[109] Ibid., 7:16.
[110] Ibid., 7:27.
[111] Narrated by Muslim in *al-Ṣaḥīḥ: Kitāb al-īmān* [Book of Faith], 1:66 §43.

through the obedience of the Prophet ﷺ and following his example. Allah ﷻ says:

مَّن يُطِعِ ٱلرَّسُولَ فَقَدْ أَطَاعَ ٱللَّهَ وَمَن تَوَلَّىٰ فَمَآ أَرْسَلْنَٰكَ عَلَيْهِمْ حَفِيظًا.

> Whoever obeys the Messenger (ﷺ) obeys (but) Allah indeed, but he who turns away, then We have not sent you to watch over them.[112]

If *īmān* is a body, the love and obedience of the Prophet ﷺ is its soul. Every effort carried out in the name of *īmān* is fruitless without love and obedience of the Messenger ﷺ just like a body without a soul. It's only the soul that leaves the body. All the organs and limbs, the ears, eyes, nose, hands and feet do not leave it. But we don't call it a human being after the soul has left. It is now a 'corpse'. Such is the case with our deeds. If all our deeds remain established while the love and obedience of the Prophet ﷺ are taken out, it is as if *īmān* has lost its soul. Ṣalāh, Zakat, Ṣawm, Hajj, *daʿwa* and all other deeds are corpses of worship if they are empty of love and reverence for the Messenger ﷺ, which we carry upon our shoulders like coffins.

Q.99. What is the pivot of *Īmān*?

Ans. The very person of the Prophet Muhammad ﷺ is the pivot of *īmān*. The stronger and more stable the connection with the Prophet ﷺ, the more perfect *īmān* is. The weaker it grows, the more deficient and incomplete *īmān* grows. If this connection breaks off, *īmān* dies. Allah ﷻ says:

---

[112] Qurʾān 4:80.

فَٱلَّذِينَ ءَامَنُواْ بِهِۦ وَعَزَّرُوهُ وَنَصَرُوهُ وَٱتَّبَعُواْ ٱلنُّورَ ٱلَّذِىٓ أُنزِلَ مَعَهُۥٓ ۙ أُوْلَٰٓئِكَ هُمُ ٱلْمُفْلِحُونَ.

> So those who will believe in this (most exalted Messenger) and will venerate and revere him and serve and support him (in his *dīn* [Religion]) and follow this light (the Qur'ān) that has been sent down with him, it is they who will flourish and prosper.'[113]

The pivot of the whole *Dīn* including faith, knowledge, cognizance, deeds and *daʿwa* is the highly esteemed person of the Prophet Muhammad ﷺ. The whole life of a believer revolves around him ﷺ.

Q.100. What role does Minhaj-ul-Quran play in the course of strengthening the *Īmān* of the Muslim Umma?

Ans. Right now, the Muslim Umma is moving rapidly towardsthe last extent of an all-embracing tribulation. Under the circumstances, it is quite natural for the Umma to be uneasy and restless for their revival and yearn for a renascence. A two-hundred-year long tribulation has created a feeling that they would have to mend their ways if they were to survive as a dignified and sovereign community on the surface of Earth. They would have to adopt the servility to our Creator ﷻ and servitude to the Prophet ﷺ. Minhaj-ul-Quran is a response to this call. It reflects the very yearning of the Muslim Umma for their renascence and the very same unease for the revival of

---

[113] Ibid., 7:157.

Islam. It upholds the banner of love and care beyond sectarian prejudices.

In order to establish and strengthen the relationship of the Umma to Allah ﷻ and His Messenger ﷺ so as to reform their affairs and train them, Minhaj-ul-Quran works under three headings.

1. Relationship with Allah ﷻ:

In our materialistic times, the relationship of servitude to and true worship of Allah ﷻ has weakened for several reasons. This has caused theological, moral and spiritual defects. The flaw in a person's spiritual state gradually penetrates the whole of society. In order to redress the problem and reinstate divine love, worship and awe, the *dhikr* gatherings are held from unit to district to province level. Also, during Ramadan, collective *iʿtikāf* (seclusion during the last ten days of Ramadan) is arranged on a huge scale for spiritual awakening, where those in attendance satiate their souls in awe and worship of Allah ﷻ as well as in love of the Messenger ﷺ. It is the third largest *iʿtikāf* gathering in the Islamic world after Mecca and Medina.

2. Relationship with the Messenger ﷺ:

Forming a heartfelt relationship with the Prophet ﷺ is actual *īmān*. In our times, our relationship of servility to him ﷺ has grown weak, and this has distanced us from our actual destination. The strength of faith lies latent within the strength of our sincere relationship of service to the Messenger ﷺ. The extreme love of the Prophet ﷺ must make this relationship a state of our heart and soul rather than just words.

As an effective measure for the love and reverence of the Messenger ﷺ to thrive, Minhaj-ul-Quran holds the gatherings of *naʿt* (enchanting praise of the Prophet ﷺ—

particularly in poetry). The activity also includes extensive spiritual training camps. A magnificent international *mawlid* festival is organised on the twelfth night of the month of Rabīᶜ al-Awwal, which is instrumental in increasing the sentimental attachment of our youth to the Prophet ﷺ.

3. Return to the Qurʾān:

The exact diagnosis of every ailment of the Umma in our times and finding a suitable remedy for each is one of the distinctions of Minhaj-ul-Quran. Deviation from the living guidance of the Qurʾān is a malady that has claimed the identity of the Umma and too much of its dignity. To address the problem, Minhaj-ul-Quran has established a network of weekly and monthly circles of lectures for Qurʾānic learning which attract large gatherings all over